Day Wa
Devon

20 circular routes in
south-west England

Vertebrate Publishing, Sheffield
www.v-publishing.co.uk

Day Walks in Devon

Devon

20 circular routes in
south-west England

Written by
Jen & Sim Benson

Day Walks in Devon
Devon

20 circular routes in south-west England

 First published in 2017 by **Vertebrate Publishing**.

Vertebrate Publishing, Crescent House, 228 Psalter Lane,
Sheffield S11 8UT, United Kingdom.
www.v-publishing.co.uk

Copyright © 2017 Jen and Sim Benson and Vertebrate Graphics Ltd.

Jen and Sim Benson have asserted their rights under the Copyright, Designs
and Patents Act 1988 to be identified as authors of this work.

A CIP catalogue record for this book is available from the British Library.

ISBN 978-1-910240-97-7

Front cover: Peartree Cove, near Start Point (route 20).
Back cover: Beer (route 12).
Photography by **Jen and Sim Benson** unless otherwise credited.

 All maps reproduced by permission of Ordnance Survey on behalf
of The Controller of Her Majesty's Stationery Office.
© Crown Copyright. 100025218

Design by Nathan Ryder, production by Jane Beagley.
www.**v-publishing**.co.uk

Printed and bound in Europe by Pulsio.
Vertebrate Publishing is committed to printing on paper from sustainable sources.

MIX
Paper from
responsible sources
FSC® C128169

Contents

VIEW SOUTH FROM BRAT TOR (ROUTE 13)

Introduction

The county of Devon spans south-west England from the Bristol Channel in the north to the English Channel in the south. To its west lies Cornwall, and to the east, Dorset and Somerset. There's so much to explore here, from the wilds of Dartmoor and Exmoor through Mid Devon's rolling green hills to the South West Coast Path that rises and falls with the rugged cliffs, hidden beaches and wooded valleys where the land meets the sea.

The name 'Devon' derives from Dumnonia, the homeland of the Dumnonii Brittonic Celts during Iron Age, Roman and early medieval Britain. Inhabitants of Dumnonia were known as *Defnas* or *Dyfneint* (deep valley dwellers).

Devon's economy is predominantly agriculture and tourism, both thriving due to its relatively mild climate and low population density. The 630-mile South West Coast Path runs along both north and south coasts with their impressive cliffs and interesting geology, interspersed with a mixture of sand and pebble beaches, fishing villages, seaside resorts and bays.

Dartmoor is the reason many walkers choose to visit Devon. At 368 square miles (954km²), it's southern England's largest open space. This vast, peat-moorland-covered granite plateau, punctuated with towering rocky tors, is the site of southern England's only mountain: High Willhays, at 621 metres. There are many fascinating historical sites and settlements scattered across the moor, and many of the small towns and villages are well worth a visit. At the time of writing, Dartmoor is the focus of much debate on the subject of rewilding; we watch with interest to see how this important area of conservation develops.

Below Dartmoor lie the South Hams, where rolling countryside and wooded river valleys are edged with picturesque coastline dotted with pretty towns and villages. Into East Devon, along the peaceful Exe estuary, to pebbled heathlands and the dramatic, fossil-strewn Jurassic Coast. Further north, Exmoor contrasts high expanses of wilderness with steep, wooded valleys and stunning coastline. You'll find wonderful views straight from the moor across the Bristol Channel to the Gower Peninsula on a clear day. Lundy, the largest island in the Channel, lies twelve miles off the North Devon coast. It's a great place to visit – as a day trip or longer – for walks, sea-cliff climbing and interesting wildlife.

Devon's many rivers, including the Exe, the Culm, the Teign, the Otter and the Dart, make for some glorious valley and riverside walking. A successful project to reintroduce the formerly native Eurasian beaver to the River Otter in 2015 means these fascinating mammals can now be seen wild in East Devon. Other highlights of the county include North Devon's UNESCO Biosphere Reserve and the Cornwall and West Devon Mining Landscape.

It certainly presented us with a sizeable challenge to pick just twenty walks to represent such a diverse and interesting county that we know and love so well, but it was a task that also brought us a lot of joy. We've gone for a mixture of local classics and lesser-known excursions and, in doing so, hope to include something to suit everyone while showcasing the very best bits of Devon.

Jen & Sim Benson

Acknowledgements

Thank you to Chris and Clare Benson for route testing and feedback and, as always, E & H for keeping us company on our adventures.

About the walks

The walks described in this book are between 8.8 and 17.6 miles (14.1 and 28.3km) in length and will take four to eight hours to complete at a leisurely pace. They will take you over a great variety of terrain and through many different landscapes.

For the most part the walks follow clear tracks and paths, waymarked routes and quiet country lanes with straightforward route finding and navigation. Some of the higher, more remote areas however, such as Dartmoor and Exmoor, can be tricky to navigate in poor visibility. While we have aimed to describe the routes in sufficient detail to follow easily when landmarks are visible, we would strongly recommend prior studying of the route, and navigational equipment appropriate to the route and conditions.

Walk times

Walk times should allow you to complete the walk at a pace that's comfortable for most regular walkers, allowing you time to enjoy the views and the occasional photo stop. Bear in mind that in the event of bad weather, getting lost, or ending up walking in the dark, these times can be extended considerably.

Navigation

Our aim is that the maps and directions in this book provide sufficient information to allow you to complete each walk. In case you need to change your plans along the way, however, it's always worth carrying a compass and the relevant OS or Harvey map(s) – and ensuring you have the skills to use them.

The routes in this book are covered by the following maps:
Ordnance Survey Explorer OL9, Exmoor (1:25,000)
Ordnance Survey Explorer OL20, South Devon (1:25,000)
Ordnance Survey Explorer OL28, Dartmoor (1:25,000)
Ordnance Survey Explorer 112, Launceston & Holsworthy (1:25,000)
Ordnance Survey Explorer 113, Okehampton (1:25,000)
Ordnance Survey Explorer 114, Exeter & the Exe Valley (1:25,000)
Ordnance Survey Explorer 115, Exmouth & Sidmouth (1:25,000)
Ordnance Survey Explorer 116, Lyme Regis & Bridport (1:25,000)
Ordnance Survey Explorer 126, Clovelly & Hartland (1:25,000)
Ordnance Survey Explorer 127, South Molton & Chulmleigh (1:25,000)
Ordnance Survey Explorer 128, Taunton & Blackdown Hills (1:25,000)
Ordnance Survey Explorer 139, Bideford, Ilfracombe & Barnstaple (1:25,000)
Harvey Superwalker, Dartmoor North (1:25,000)
Harvey Superwalker, Dartmoor South (1:25,000)
Harvey British Mountain Map, Dartmoor (1:40,000)

The majority but not all of the coastal routes are also covered by the Harvey National
Trail series below:
Harvey National Trail, South West Coast Path 1 (1:40,000)
Harvey National Trail, South West Coast Path 3 (1:40,000)

GPS
A GPS device can be a useful backup and great for checking route data. Take spare batteries
and never rely on one as your sole method of navigation.

Mobile phones
A mobile phone is well worth taking in case you – or anyone else you meet on your walk
– need emergency assistance. Conserve battery life as much as possible or take a spare
'emergencies only' phone if you like to post live updates as you go.

footpaths and rights of way

All of the routes in this book follow rights of way, permissive paths or cross open access land.

Comfort

Well-fitting boots or approach shoes with good grip protect you and your feet as you walk. Waterproof footwear is a good idea in wet conditions. A lightweight waterproof will pack easily into a rucksack but provide warmth and protection should you need it. In very poor weather take enough clothing with you that, should you need to stop, you can still keep warm. Spare clothing, food and drink will all help to make your walk enjoyable.

Safety

For the most part, the Devon climate makes for pleasant walking conditions year round. However, specific areas can experience very challenging conditions, so it's worth checking the forecast before you set out and planning – or postponing – accordingly. Dartmoor gets more than its fair share of rain and the rivers running from the moor fill rapidly and may become difficult to cross. The higher areas of the moor, around Princetown, often see snowfall in winter. Similarly, Exmoor has many high, remote areas that become hard work, both physically and from a navigation point of view, in poor weather. Take care with high winds, big tides and cliff erosion in coastal areas; some sections of the South West Coast Path have been rerouted inland where their original course has been claimed by the sea. It's always worth carrying basic emergency items: survival blanket, whistle, first aid kit, torch and mobile phone.

Rescue

In the case of an emergency dial **999** and ask for **Police** and then **Search and Rescue.** If you need the **Coastguard**, dial **999** or **112** and ask for the **Coastguard**. Where possible give a six-figure grid reference of your location or that of your casualty. If you don't have mobile reception try to attract the attention of others nearby. The standard distress signal is six short blasts on a whistle every minute.

Emergency rescue by SMS text

In the UK you can also contact the emergency services by SMS text – useful if you have low battery or intermittent signal. You need to register your phone first by texting **'register'** to 999 and then following the instructions in the reply. **Do it now** – it could save yours or someone else's life. **www.emergencysms.org.uk**

Military firing

Walk 13, Brat Tor & High Willhays on Dartmoor, ventures into an area where the Ministry of Defence carries out live firing exercises. A comprehensive list of maps and times can be found online here: **www.gov.uk/government/publications/dartmoor-firing-programme** Please check the times before you leave for your walk, and if the red flags are flying when you approach the range do not enter.

Walk 11, Woodbury, also passes near to a live firing range. Firing times are posted here: **www.gov.uk/government/publications/straightpoint-and-wcta-grenade-range-firing-times** – Do not enter the area when the red flags are flying.

TRACK BETWEEN YES TOR AND HIGH WILLHAYS (ROUTE 13)

The Countryside Code

Respect other people
Please respect the local community and other people using the outdoors. Remember your actions can affect people's lives and livelihoods.

Consider the local community and other people enjoying the outdoors
» Respect the needs of local people and visitors alike – for example, don't block gateways, driveways or other paths with your vehicle.
» When riding a bike or driving a vehicle, slow down or stop for horses, walkers and farm animals and give them plenty of room. By law, cyclists must give way to walkers and horse riders on bridleways.
» Co-operate with people at work in the countryside. For example, keep out of the way when farm animals are being gathered or moved and follow directions from the farmer.
» Busy traffic on small country roads can be unpleasant and dangerous to local people, visitors and wildlife – so slow down and, where possible, leave your vehicle at home, consider sharing lifts and use alternatives such as public transport or cycling. For public transport information, phone Traveline on 0871 200 22 33 or visit **www.traveline.info**

Leave gates and property as you find them and follow paths unless wider access is available
» A farmer will normally close gates to keep farm animals in, but may sometimes leave them open so the animals can reach food and water. Leave gates as you find them or follow instructions on signs. When in a group, make sure the last person knows how to leave the gates.
» Follow paths unless wider access is available, such as on open country or registered common land (known as 'open access' land).
» If you think a sign is illegal or misleading such as a *Private – No Entry* sign on a public path, contact the local authority.
» Leave machinery and farm animals alone – don't interfere with animals even if you think they're in distress. Try to alert the farmer instead.
» Use gates, stiles or gaps in field boundaries if you can – climbing over walls, hedges and fences can damage them and increase the risk of farm animals escaping.
» Our heritage matters to all of us – be careful not to disturb ruins and historic sites.

Protect the natural environment

We all have a responsibility to protect the countryside now and for future generations, so make sure you don't harm animals, birds, plants or trees and try to leave no trace of your visit. When out with your dog make sure it is not a danger or nuisance to farm animals, horses, wildlife or other people.

Leave no trace of your visit and take your litter home

» Protecting the natural environment means taking special care not to damage, destroy or remove features such as rocks, plants and trees. They provide homes and food for wildlife, and add to everybody's enjoyment of the countryside.

» Litter and leftover food doesn't just spoil the beauty of the countryside, it can be dangerous to wildlife and farm animals – so take your litter home with you. Dropping litter and dumping rubbish are criminal offences.

» Fires can be as devastating to wildlife and habitats as they are to people and property – so be careful with naked flames and cigarettes at any time of the year. Sometimes, controlled fires are used to manage vegetation, particularly on heaths and moors between 1 October and 15 April, but if a fire appears to be unattended then report it by calling **999**.

Keep dogs under effective control

When you take your dog into the outdoors, always ensure it does not disturb wildlife, farm animals, horses or other people by keeping it under effective control. This means that you:

» keep your dog on a lead, or

» keep it in sight at all times, be aware of what it's doing and be confident it will return to you promptly on command

» ensure it does not stray off the path or area where you have a right of access

Special dog rules may apply in particular situations, so always look out for local signs – for example:

» dogs may be banned from certain areas that people use, or there may be restrictions, byelaws or control orders limiting where they can go

» the access rights that normally apply to open country and registered common land (known as 'open access' land) require dogs to be kept on a short lead between 1 March and 31 July, to help protect ground-nesting birds, and all year round near farm animals

» at the coast, there may also be some local restrictions to require dogs to be kept on a short lead during the bird breeding season, and to prevent disturbance to flocks of resting and feeding birds during other times of year

It's always good practice (and a legal requirement on 'open access' land) to keep your dog on a lead around farm animals and horses, for your own safety and for the welfare of the animals. A farmer may shoot a dog which is attacking or chasing farm animals without being liable to compensate the dog's owner.

However, if cattle or horses chase you and your dog, it is safer to let your dog off the lead – don't risk getting hurt by trying to protect it. Your dog will be much safer if you let it run away from a farm animal in these circumstances and so will you.

Everyone knows how unpleasant dog mess is and it can cause infections, so always clean up after your dog and get rid of the mess responsibly – 'bag it and bin it'. Make sure your dog is wormed regularly to protect it, other animals and people.

Enjoy the outdoors
Even when going out locally, it's best to get the latest information about where and when you can go. For example, your rights to go on to some areas of open access land and coastal land may be restricted in particular places at particular times. Find out as much as you can about where you are going, plan ahead and follow advice and local signs.

Plan ahead and be prepared
You'll get more from your visit if you refer to up-to-date maps or guidebooks and websites before you go. Visit **www.gov.uk/natural-england** or contact local information centres or libraries for a list of outdoor recreation groups offering advice on specialist activities.

You're responsible for your own safety and for others in your care – especially children – so be prepared for natural hazards, changes in weather and other events. Wild animals, farm animals and horses can behave unpredictably if you get too close, especially if they're with their young – so give them plenty of space.

Check weather forecasts before you leave. Conditions can change rapidly especially on mountains and along the coast, so don't be afraid to turn back. When visiting the coast check for tide times on **www.ukho.gov.uk/easytide** – don't risk getting cut off by rising tides and take care on slippery rocks and seaweed.

Part of the appeal of the countryside is that you can get away from it all. You may not see anyone for hours, and there are many places without clear mobile phone signals, so let someone else know where you're going and when you expect to return.

Follow advice and local signs
England has about 190,000km (118,000 miles) of public rights of way, providing many opportunities to enjoy the natural environment. Get to know the signs and symbols used in the countryside to show paths and open countryside.

PRAWLE POINT FROM LANGERSTONE POINT (ROUTE 20)

How to use this book

This book should provide you with all of the information that you need for an enjoyable, trouble-free and successful walk. The following tips should also be of help:

» We strongly recommend that you invest in the relevant map listed above on page ix. These are essential even if you are familiar with the area – you may need to cut short the walk or take an alternative route.

» Choose your route. Consider the time you have available and the abilities/level of experience of all members of your party – then read the Safety section of this guide.

» We recommend that you study the route description carefully before setting off. Cross-reference this with your map so that you've got a good sense of general orientation in case you need an escape route. Make sure that you are familiar with the symbols used on the maps.

» Get out there and get walking!

BEER BEACH FROM THE SOUTH WEST COAST PATH (ROUTE 12)

Maps, descriptions, distances

While every effort has been made to maintain accuracy within the maps and descriptions in this guide, we have had to process a vast amount of information and we are unable to guarantee that every single detail is correct. Please exercise caution if a direction appears at odds with the route on the map. If in doubt, a comparison between the route, the description and a quick cross-reference with your map (along with a bit of common sense) should help ensure that you're on the right track. Note that distances have been measured off the map, and map distances rarely coincide 100 per cent with distances on the ground. Please treat stated distances as a guideline only.

Ordnance Survey maps are the most commonly used, are easy to read and many people are happy using them. If you're not familiar with OS maps and are unsure of what the symbols mean, you can download a free OS 1:25,000 map legend from **www.ordnancesurvey.co.uk**

Here are a few of the symbols and abbreviations we use on the maps and in our directions:

 ROUTE STARTING POINT   ROUTE MARKER   SHORTCUT

 OPTIONAL ROUTE   ADDITIONAL GRID LINE NUMBERS TO AID NAVIGATION

PB = public bridleway
GR = grid reference
RHS/RH = Right-hand side/Right-hand

PF = public footpath
LHS/LH = Left-hand side/Left-hand
SWCP = South West Coast Path

Km/mile conversion chart

Metric to Imperial

1 kilometre [km]	1,000 m	0.6214 mile
1 metre [m]	100 cm	1.0936 yd
1 centimetre [cm]	10 mm	0.3937 in
1 millimetre [mm]		0.03937 in

Imperial to Metric

1 mile	1,760 yd	1.6093 km
1 yard [yd]	3 ft	0.9144 m
1 foot [ft]	12 in	0.3048 m
1 inch [in]		2.54 cm

Lundy

Barn

Bidef

Hartland Point **5**

Hartland

Kilkhampton

Bude Stratto

Cornwall

Boscastle

Tintagel

Launcesto

Port Isaac

Camelford

Padstow

Bodmin Moor

Calling

Wadebridge

CORNWALL

Bodmin

Lisk

Bugle

Lostwithiel

St Austell

Looe

Fowey

Polperro

Whit

Probus

Mevagissey

Cornwall

Dodman
Point

St Mawes

nouth

uth Bay

Day Walks in
Devon
Area Map & Route Finder

North Devon & Exmoor

This section explores the rugged North Devon coast, an Area of Outstanding Natural Beauty and home to many fascinating examples of Devonian geology. Sandy beaches intersperse airy headlands and much of the best walking follows the South West Coast Path. Heading inland, the 180-mile Tarka Trail loops the peaceful lanes, fields and woods of the North Devon countryside.

Exmoor National Park straddles the Devon/ Somerset border, stretching southwards from its rugged coastal edge at the Bristol Channel. The walking here is wonderfully diverse, from wild and windswept high moorland to steep-sided wooded valleys that follow tumbling streams from the moor to the sea.

SOUTH WEST COAST PATH TO THE VALLEY OF ROCKS (ROUTE 2)

BAGGY POINT

Baggy Point   20.2km/12.6miles

An enjoyable coastal walk taking in dramatic rocky headlands and some of North Devon's most famous surfing beaches.

Baggy Point car park » Croyde beach » Saunton » Croyde » Woolacombe Down » Woolacombe » Woolacombe Sand » Putsborough Sand » Baggy Point » Baggy Point car park

Start

Baggy Point National Trust car park. GR: SS 432397.

The Walk

A buzzing surfing and family holiday hotspot in the summer, yet peaceful and windswept in winter, Croyde Bay is an enjoyable place to visit at any time of year. The golden, sandy crescent is edged with rocky, pool-filled plateaus, fascinating cliffs and high dunes. This section of the coast is a Site of Special Scientific Interest due to its important geology and geomorphology, and also part of the North Devon Coast Area of Outstanding Natural Beauty.

Our walk begins at Croyde Bay, crossing the beach and following the South West Coast Path around Saunton Down with views across to Saunton Sands and Braunton Burrows. Turning inland we climb over the grassy headland above Saunton before descending steeply to walk through Croyde itself. Rejoining the coast path, we head along Woolacombe Down with views of the three-mile stretch of sand along Woolacombe Bay.

On our return trip we descend to the beach and follow it around to Putsborough Sand, with entertainment provided by the many surfers who brave the waves here. Leaving the beach we once again rejoin the coast path, following it to the rocky headland and series of outcrops at Baggy Point. This area is a haven for wildlife, and stonechats flit between the coconut-scented gorse bushes in summer. Baggy Point's vast slabs of Devonian sandstone, which slope down to wave-washed rocky platforms, are popular with climbers and there are several classic routes here. The views from the top are extensive, across the water to Lundy, north along the coast to Morte Point beyond Woolacombe, and back past Croyde to the Hartland Peninsula.

From Baggy Point we follow wide, gorse-lined paths back to Croyde Bay – the cream teas at Sandleigh Tea Rooms are highly recommended.

BAGGY POINT

DISTANCE: 20.2KM/12.6MILES » **TOTAL ASCENT:** 479M/1,572FT » **START GR:** SS 432397 » **TIME:** ALLOW 5.5 HOURS » **SATNAV:** EX33 1PA » **MAP:** OS EXPLORER 139, BIDEFORD, ILFRACOMBE AND BARNSTAPLE, 1:25,000 » **REFRESHMENTS:** SANDLEIGH TEA ROOMS, CROYDE BAY » **NAVIGATION:** STRAIGHTFORWARD PATHS AND LANES.

Woolacombe

Barricane Beach

Grunta Pool

Hotel

Hotel

PO

Sports

Water Works

Popper's Hill

Woolacombe Down

Pickwell

West Glyn

Mill Rock

Marine Drive

Tarka Trail

South West Coast Path

Woolacombe Warren

Woolacombe Sand

Mean Low Water

Morte Bay

Wheeler's Stone

Black Rock

42

01 BAGGY POINT

Directions – Baggy Point

❺► **Turn left** out of the car park and walk for a short section along the road until you can **turn right** down a slipway on to the rocks at the edge of Croyde beach (if the tide is high you may need to carry on further along the road before turning on to the beach or carry on further and join the South West Coast Path (SWCP) from the road). Cross the rocks and the beach aiming for the south-eastern corner where you can join the SWCP in the dunes. **Turn right** on to the SWCP and follow it parallel to the road around the headland. Cross the B3231 and continue on the SWCP heading east following the road. Follow the SWCP as it turns left and heads uphill away from the road and then curves right contouring the hill to reach the end of a lane above Saunton.

2 **Turn left** here leaving the SWCP and heading north on a footpath uphill to the high point of this headland. Follow the path down the other side of the hill. The path becomes a track and then joins Milkaway Lane. **Turn left** here and then take the **second left** joining Cloutman's Lane. Follow this into Croyde to reach the B3231 (Hobb's Hill). **Turn right** on the B3231 and then **left** on to Jones's Hill, signed *Baggy Point* and *Croyde Beach*. Follow this road north and continue uphill on to Stentaway Lane, signed *Putsborough Beach*. **Turn left** where the road takes a sharp right bend and follow the dead-end lane signed *Cherry Tree Farm*.

3 Follow this lane uphill until it turns sharply left. **Turn right** here on to a footpath going east at the top of the hill. Follow this to join the SWCP above Putsborough Sand. **Turn left** on to the lane here and follow it as it turns into a track. Follow the SWCP and bridleway signs towards Woolacombe. After about 1km at a path junction take the **left fork** following SWCP signs down some steps and into the dunes. **Turn right** on to a path following the SWCP signs north through the dunes until you reach a road.

4 **Turn left** and follow Challacombe Hill Road towards Woolacombe. After 200m **turn left** on to the beach and follow the sands south back towards Baggy Point. When you reach Putsborough Sand leave the beach, passing the car park and heading steeply uphill back to the road that you followed briefly on the outbound route. **Turn right** and follow the road until you can **turn right** through a gate and on to the SWCP.

5 Follow the well-signed SWCP west along the northern edge of Baggy Point. As you reach the end the path curves to the left and drops down to the south-western corner. A **sharp left** here and you continue on the SWCP but now heading south-east along a good track on the southern edge of the promontory. Follow this path until you reach a small lane; **turn right** here and follow it back to the car park at the start of the route.

CROYDE BAY

WOODY BAY FROM THE EAST

Heddon Valley & Lynton 21.2km/13.2miles

Explore craggy coastal cliffs and the dry bed of a long-lost river before diving down into the depths of a deep, wooded valley.

The Valley of Rocks » Castle Rock » Crock Point » Woody Bay » Highveer Point » Heddon Valley » Hunters Inn » The Beacon » Slattenslade » Croscombe Barton » Valley of Rocks south ridge » Lynton » North Walk » The Valley of Rocks

Start
The Valley of Rocks car park.
GR: SS 707497.

The Walk
The Valley of Rocks was once the course of a great river; a river that carved the deep groove that runs from the western edge of Lynton down towards the sea at Lee Bay. The valley now lies high and dry, surrounded by towering rock sculptures and the rolling Exmoor hills. Perhaps due to glacial retreat or erosion by the sea, there's still no one clear answer to the mystery of the missing river.

Our walk starts in the heart of the Valley of Rocks, just below the fortress of Castle Rock with its fine views across the Bristol Channel to Wales. Taking to the South West Coast Path, we walk through dramatic cliff-edged moorland and along narrow, winding trails high above the waves. This part of the coast is a Site of Special Scientific Interest because of its rare lichens, trees and wildlife.

Diving down into Heddon Valley we follow the tranquil River Heddon upstream as it makes its way off Exmoor to the sea at Heddon's Mouth. There's an opportunity for refreshments at the Hunters Inn, which lies nestled at the valley's edge, before we head back up the steep track to reach the higher path on which we return. Glorious views await as the route winds between wild open moorland and the sea.

Following a route along the southern edge of the Valley of Rocks we descend steeply into the village of Lynton with views down to Lynmouth beyond. If you have time to spare, catch the famous funicular cliff railway down to Lynmouth and back, crossing our route at North Walk on its way.

We finish our walk with a fine stretch of coast path that leaves Lynton and traverses the cliff edges, winding its way at half-height through goat-grazed crags to return to the Valley of Rocks.

HEDDON VALLEY & LYNTON

DISTANCE: 21.2KM/13.2MILES » **TOTAL ASCENT:** 1,003M/3,291FT » **START GR:** SS 707497 » **TIME:** ALLOW 7 HOURS » **SATNAV:** EX35 6JH » **MAP:** OS EXPLORER OL9, EXMOOR, 1:25,000 » **REFRESHMENTS:** HUNTERS INN, HEDDON VALLEY; CHARLIE FRIDAY'S, LYNTON » **NAVIGATION:** EASY-TO-FOLLOW PATHS AND LANES.

LOOKING EAST FROM MARTINHOE

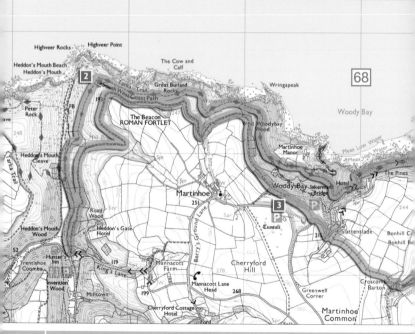

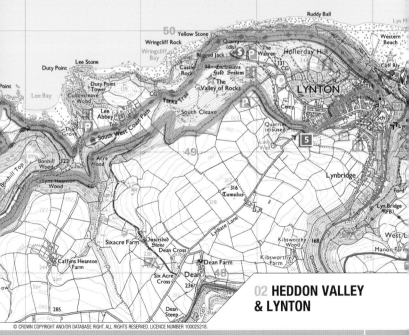

02 HEDDON VALLEY & LYNTON

Directions – Heddon Valley & Lynton

➎▶ **Turn right** out of the car park and follow the road for a short section to join the South West Coast Path below Castle Rock. Follow the SWCP as it runs south-west along the road, downhill initially and then uphill above Lee Bay. **Turn right** off the road, following the SWCP which runs around Crock Point before returning to the road. **Turn right**, following the road and **forking right** at the junction. Take the **right turn** on to the coast path again and follow it through woodland around Woody Bay and then out on to the coastal moorland. Follow the precipitous cliff path around Highveer Point and inland into Heddon Valley.

2 The coast path drops downhill and follows the river upstream to reach the road at the Hunters Inn. **Turn back on yourself** and follow the higher track uphill through woodland towards the sea. The track contours around the coast near the top of the hill, heading generally eastwards to reach a road above Woody Bay.

3 **Turn right** on the road and follow it into Slattenslade. Cross the stream and then **turn right** on to a footpath heading south-east across some fields to Croscombe Barton. Continue on the path, cross the stream, then **turn left** and follow the track on the east side of the stream to reach a small bridge.

4 **Don't** cross the bridge; **turn right** on to the footpath and continue on the east bank of the river, taking the **right-hand fork** after about 1km and then reaching a larger track which is a bridleway. **Turn right** on to this and follow it to the next sharp corner. **Continue ahead** in the same direction here on a footpath across moorland, taking the **right-hand** path uphill and then **turning left** across the moor above the Valley of Rocks. Follow the path downhill and right through some woods to reach a road above Lynton.

5 **Turn left** on to Lydiate Lane and head downhill, then **left** and then **right** on to Lee Road. Follow this through town then **turn left** on to North Walk just before the church. Follow North Walk to its end where it becomes the SWCP. Follow this spectacular section of the SWCP back to the Valley of Rocks. Leave the SWCP and **turn left** on to the road and back to the car park.

LYNMOUTH

BRENDON COMMON

03 Foreland Point & the Doone Valley

22.6km/14miles

An adventurous walk that takes in wild and windswept high moor, rugged coastal trails and the northernmost point of Devon.

Countisbury » East Lyn River » Rockford » Shilstone » Shilstone Hill » Lank Combe » Badgworthy Water » Cloud Farm » Malmsmead » County Gate » SW Coast Path » Foreland Point » Countisbury

Start

National Trust car park at Countisbury. GR: SS 752496.

The Walk

Our walk starts at Countisbury, a village that lies on the route of the infamous lifeboat rescue of 1899. One stormy night, unable to launch from Lynmouth, a team of local residents and twenty horses hauled the lifeboat fourteen miles up and over Exmoor to assist a stricken vessel off the coast of Porlock.

From Countisbury we drop down into the deep gorge at Watersmeet, the confluence of the East Lyn River and Hoar Oak Water, following the Coleridge Way along the winding wooded valley. We climb to the summit of Shilstone Hill, where the remains of three WWII practice slit trenches are visible from the air and two standing stones mark a former peat harvesting site. The ascent to the trig point is rewarded with great views out across the Bristol Channel.

Crossing the empty wilderness of Brendon Common into Doone Country, the grassy moor slopes steeply down to Badgworthy Water. We follow the river's course through the ancient woodland of the Doone Valley, passing the R.D. Blackmore memorial just before Cloud Farm. From here the climb is steep up to County Gate, the border between Devon and Somerset – look behind you for glorious views of the East Lyn Valley and Doone Country. Now we rejoin the South West Coast Path, heading through woodland before emerging on to the clifftops for fine walking above Countisbury Cove.

Foreland Point marks the northernmost tip of Devon and is a wonderful place to watch the sun set – the National Trust-owned bothy right on the coast path is a perfect viewing point and an enjoyable alternative to camping. Finally, leaving Foreland behind, we climb back up and over Butter Hill to finish at Countisbury.

FORELAND POINT & THE DOONE VALLEY

DISTANCE: 22.6KM/14MILES » **TOTAL ASCENT:** 973M/3,192FT » **START GR:** SS 752496 » **TIME:** ALLOW 7 HOURS » **SATNAV:** EX35 6NE (NEAREST) » **MAP:** OS EXPLORER OL9, EXMOOR, 1:25,000 » **REFRESHMENTS:** NATIONAL TRUST CAFE AT WATERSMEET (SEASONAL); THE BLUE BALL INN, COUNTISBURY » **NAVIGATION:** MAINLY CLEAR PATHS BUT CORRECT PATH CHOICE ON THE MOORLAND AREAS CAN BE HARD IN POOR VISIBILITY.

03 FORELAND POINT & THE DOONE VALLEY

Directions – Foreland Point & the Doone Valley

➏ From the car park cross the A39 and head **south**, downhill, on a bridleway which contours to the left. **Turn right** on to a footpath just before the second small stream crossing and follow this west, downhill, to the East Lyn River. **Turn left** and follow the river upstream, crossing on the footbridge and joining the road just beyond the Rockford Inn. **Turn left** on to the road and follow it upstream for a short section before **turning right** on to a footpath opposite a house, heading uphill into some woods.

2 Follow the path through the woods to the next road. **Turn left** on to the road and follow it downhill and then up to a sharp left turn. Take the footpath on the **right** at the bend, over a stile into a field and follow the path uphill to the track. **Turn right** on the track through Shilstone and then **right again** on to the path just past the buildings. Follow the path across the stream and uphill in a southerly direction to the trig point on Shilstone Hill.

3 Continue on the path south and then **fork left**, cutting the corner that would other-wise take you to the road at Dry Bridge. **Turn left** at the next path junction and follow the track north-east initially. **Stay right** at the next fork and continue on the main track. After about 400m take a smaller path **right** crossing a stream at Lankcombe Ford and heading downhill in a south-easterly direction. Cross a fence and then **fork left** to reach the path running along Badgworthy Water.

4 **Turn left** and follow the bridleway down the river and through woodland. Cross the river at the footbridge by Cloud Farm campsite and then **turn left** and follow the farm track to the road at Malmsmead. **Turn right** on the road and follow it uphill for a short section until you can **turn left** on to a bridleway which crosses the river. **Turn left** after the bridge and follow the river downstream for about 500m. The path here turns **sharply right** – follow it but **don't** take the next left; instead **continue ahead** steeply uphill to reach the A39 at County Gate car park.

5 Cross the road and follow the path north, downhill, into some woods to join the South West Coast Path. **Turn left** on to the SWCP and follow it through woodland and then out on to the coast in a generally westward direction. Continue on the SWCP until you can **fork right** down a metalled road past the National Trust bothy to reach Foreland Point lighthouse.

6 From the lighthouse continue on the coastal path heading south-west and rejoining the signed South West Coast Path. Follow this around Butter Hill to reach a path junction just north of Countisbury; **turn left** here following the path south-east back to the car park.

CODDOW COMBE AND THE NATIONAL TRUST BOTHY PHOTO: ROB JOULES

EGGESFORD CHURCH

Chulmleigh on the Tarka Trail 17.3km/10.7miles

Explore the quiet lanes, rivers and footpaths of deepest North Devon, through an area of rural tranquillity rich in wildlife.

Chulmleigh » Chawleigh Week » Upcott Wood » Nethercott » Homeland Wood » Homeland Bridge » Eggesford Barton » Eggesford Fourways » Trenchard Farm » Chenson » Chawleigh » Hollow Tree Cross » Little Dart River » Chulmleigh

Start

By St Mary Magdalene Church, New Street, Chulmleigh. GR: SS 686141.

The Walk

The Chulmleigh area has been designated as both an Area of Rural Tranquillity and an Area of Great Landscape Value. It has one of the greatest concentrations of species-rich grassland – known as Culm grasslands – in the world, providing habitat for a variety of wildlife including curlews and marsh fritillary butterflies. The old hedges and copses, dating back to Saxon times, are home to dormice and the rare brown hairstreak butterfly. This area also has the largest population of wild otters in England.

We begin our walk leaving the village of Chulmleigh on the Tarka Trail. Named after Henry Williamson's novel, *Tarka the Otter*, the trail is a regular feature around North Devon, meandering through the countryside in a series of footpaths, bridleways and

cycleways. In total it spans some 180 miles, signed at intervals with an otter's pawprint.

Crossing the Little Dart River, a tributary of the main Dart that rises on Dartmoor and flows to the English Channel at Dartmouth, we walk through forestry land and the ancient wooded areas around Eggesford. There's a station here should you wish to arrive by train and join the walk at point 3.

Another river crossing – this time the Taw – takes us around in a wide loop through farmland, woodland and along inviting trails to the village of Chawleigh. Many houses in the villages in this part of Devon are still the original cob and thatch construction and thatchers can often be seen working on the roofs.

From Chawleigh we head down into the leafy river valley of the Little Dart once more, following its winding route briefly before climbing steeply back up to our finish at Chulmleigh.

CHULMLEIGH ON THE TARKA TRAIL

DISTANCE: 17.3KM/10.7MILES » **TOTAL ASCENT:** 459M/1,506FT » **START GR:** SS 686141 » **TIME:** ALLOW 5 HOURS » **SATNAV:** EX18 7BR » **MAP:** OS EXPLORER 127, SOUTH MOLTON & CHULMLEIGH, AND A VERY SMALL SECTION OF OS EXPLORER 113, OKEHAMPTON, BOTH 1:25,000 » **REFRESHMENTS:** THE RED LION, CHULMLEIGH » **NAVIGATION:** STRAIGHTFORWARD PATHS AND LANES.

FOOTBRIDGE AT POINT 8 OVER LITTLE DART

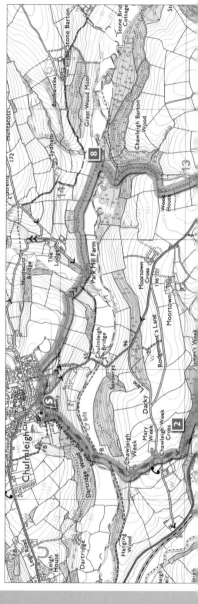

04 CHULMLEIGH ON THE TARKA TRAIL

Directions – Chulmleigh on the Tarka Trail

❺▶ With the south side of St Mary Magdalene church at your back, **turn right** along New Street and head west for a short distance, then **turn left** and head downhill on Rock Hill. Follow this lane down to the footbridge at the bottom and cross, continuing on the lane uphill to the farm. **Turn left** here and follow a lane into the small hamlet of Chawleigh Week. **Turn right** and then **left** on the road and follow it downhill through some woodland.

2 Take the **first left** turn on to a forestry track just after the left-hand bend in the road. Follow the main track through the woodland **trending right** until you reach a junction where a footpath leaves the woods on your right, the track leaves the woods in front of you and the forest track turns left. Follow the track **left** here uphill through the woods to reach the southern edge of Upcott Wood. **Turn left** and follow the track east along the edge of the wood to a field. **Turn right** across a small footbridge and then follow the path up some rough steps through woodland to the road at Nethercott Farm.

3 **Turn right** on to the road and then **left** on to a footpath across a field and through a gate. Follow the gently contouring path downhill into the valley heading south to reach the road near Eggesford Station. **Turn left** here on to the A377 and then **left again** into the forestry car park. Follow the forestry track south-east, initially parallel to the road and then swinging left and uphill to the edge of the forest. Continue on the path that follows the edge of the wood downhill to reach another main forest track. **Turn left** on to the track and then **right** on to a footpath heading downhill and back to the road.

4 Cross the A377 and follow the footpath marked *Tarka Trail and Eggesford Church* across a field, under the railway and then over the railway bridge to cross the river. **Turn right** on to a larger track, heading uphill to join the Tarka Trail at Eggesford Barton. **Turn left** here and follow the Tarka Trail uphill on the track and then **right** across some fields in a south-westerly direction to Eggesford Fourways.

5 **Turn left** on to the road and follow it until you can **turn left** into Trenchard Farm. Follow the Tarka Trail through the farmyard and down the track to reach fields above the river. Follow the footpath heading east across these fields and along the river to a track. **Turn left** on to the track leaving the Tarka Trail and follow it over the bridge to reach the A377 at Chenson.

6 Cross the A377 and follow the bridleway **left** around the back of the houses and then **right** uphill along the edge of some fields. Continue on the path, **turning right** at the corner of the wood and then joining a banked track, following this to the road below Toatley Farm. **Turn left** on to the road and then, about 100m later, **turn right** on to a footpath following the southern bank of the stream across some fields. Go through the gate on to a track and **turn left** heading uphill to a gate at the end of the road. Follow the footpath **straight ahead** across fields, trending **right** around a house to reach the road at Chawleigh.

7 **Turn left** on to the road and follow it through the village to Hollow Tree Cross. **Turn right** on to a footpath here and follow it north, downhill, across two fields ending at a track in the bottom right corner. Follow the main track downhill to a clearing where a footpath leads **right** into the trees at the bottom. Follow the footpath around to the right and through the woods then curving left to reach the footbridge (this section can be very wet but you can avoid the worst through the trees).

8 Cross the Little Dart River and follow the footpath **left** along a track, over two small footbridges and along the bottom of a field to the road. **Turn left** on to the road and follow it uphill into Chulmleigh.

PATH SOUTH OF NETHERCOTT

SECTION 2

Torridge & West Devon

This section covers the north and west of the county, from the Hartland Peninsula in the north along the Cornish border to the north-western fringes of Dartmoor. It is one of the most sparsely populated areas in Devon; green, leafy and ablaze with daffodils and primroses in spring. Peaceful woodland, riverside trails and unusual wildlife habitats provide interesting and intriguing walking. Hartland's hidden gems make for some exciting exploration. Its rugged coastline boasts ancient hill forts and iconic landmarks such as Blackchurch Rock. The entire peninsula is an Area of Outstanding Natural Beauty and part of the UNESCO North Devon Biosphere Reserve.

TARKA TRAIL BY THE RIVER TAW NORTH OF BONDLEIGH (ROUTE 8)

HARTLAND POINT LIGHTHOUSE WITH LUNDY ON THE HORIZON

05 **Hartland Point**

A tour of the classic sights to be found on the beautiful Hartland Peninsula, taking in peaceful rolling countryside and a glorious stretch of the South West Coast Path.

Hartland Quay » Damehole Point » Hartland Point » Titchberry » Beckland Bay » Windbury Point » Blackchurch Rock » Brownsham » Norton » Hartland » Hartland Abbey » Stoke » Hartland Quay

Start
Hartland Quay. GR: SS 222247.

The Walk

The Hartland Peninsula juts into the sea from the north coast of Devon, its tip marking the point where the Bristol Channel meets the Atlantic Ocean. Our walk begins at Hartland Quay, a former harbour that dates back to the time of Henry VIII. Fierce storms, common around this headland, eroded the pier over the centuries, and it eventually crumbled into the sea in 1887. Many ships have been stricken on the rocks that surround this part of the coast.

From Hartland Quay we head north along the South West Coast Path, the trail rising and falling with a series of sea cliffs until Hartland Point with its white lighthouse comes into view. There are fine views from here out across the sea to Lundy, a three-mile-long granite outcrop that lies twelve miles off the Devon coast and an enjoyable place to explore. Over the winter months the Lundy helicopter flies from Hartland Point – if you visit between October and March you might catch a glimpse of it as you walk.

Continuing onwards along the coast path, passing the Iron Age hill fort at Windbury, we drop down to Mouth Mill. On the beach here stands the great pyramid stack of Blackchurch Rock, a favourite with climbers, geologists and photographers alike.

Heading inland we walk on quiet lanes alongside high, windswept fields, skirting the village of Hartland before descending to the entrance to Hartland Abbey. This former monastery was built in 1157 and is now a family home. The house and gardens are open for members of the public to visit through the summer months (paid entry). Continuing onwards we reach the village of Stoke, whose high tower remains a significant landmark for ships in the Bristol Channel. A gentle descent brings us back to Hartland Quay.

HARTLAND POINT

DISTANCE: 21.9KM/13.6MILES » **TOTAL ASCENT:** 840M/2,756FT » **START GR:** SS 222247 » **TIME:** ALLOW 7 HOURS » **SATNAV:** EX39 6DU » **MAP:** OS EXPLORER 126, CLOVELLY & HARTLAND, 1:25,000 » **REFRESHMENTS:** LAVENDER TEA ROOMS, HIGHER CHERISTOW, HARTLAND » **NAVIGATION:** MAINLY STRAIGHTFORWARD ON COAST PATH AND LANES.

05 HARTLAND POINT

Directions – Hartland Point

➏ Join the South West Coast Path and head north along the cliffs to Hartland Point. Continue on the SWCP, now heading east past Titchberry and Chapman Rock. Continue around Beckland Bay and follow the path into some woods above Blackchurch Rock. Follow the path as it zigzags steeply downhill to Mouth Mill.

2 Cross the stream and **bear right**, leaving the SWCP and following the path inland (south), across a stream and along the edge of Snaxland Wood to reach a bridleway. **Turn right** on to the bridleway and follow it west through Brownsham Wood to reach a track and then the end of a road.

3 **Turn left** on to the road and then take the **first right** on to another lane. Follow this **straight across** the crossroads. Follow this lane for a short distance and then take the **first left** on to a track heading south-west past Norton farm to reach another lane. **Turn left** here and follow it downhill to a junction. **Turn left** downhill and then **right** at the next junction.

4 Follow the road for a short distance and then **fork left** on to a footpath, heading west through some woods. The path continues following the Abbey River but running a short distance north of it in the woods. **Continue** on to the lane at the end of the path and then **turn right** on to the road heading uphill past the entrance to Hartland Abbey. Continue up the road until you can **turn left** on to a footpath across some fields. Follow this to the next road.

5 **Turn left** on to the road and follow it downhill and across the river. **Continue** up the road and **turn right** at the junction near the church. Follow this road west past the church and then down to Hartland Quay.

SMOOTHLANDS

A glimpse into the history of the Great Torrington area, where fascinating relics lie hidden within the glorious Devon countryside.

Great Torrington station » Tarka Trail » Priestacott » Frithelstock » Monkleigh » Annery Kiln » Weare Giffard » Huntshaw Mill Bridge » Great Torrington station

Start
Great Torrington station. GR: SS 480197.

The Walk
Our walk begins at the former station in Great Torrington, along one of the paved, multi-user sections of the 180-mile Tarka Trail that loops its way in a figure of eight around North Devon. Torrington itself is a small market town set along the River Torridge. To the east of the town are 365 acres of wildlife-rich common land, donated to the town in the twelfth century. There are over twenty miles of footpaths to explore around the commons.

Leaving the Tarka Trail we climb up and over open land at Priestacott, with fine views back down across the Torridge valley. At Frithelstock (pronounced Frizzlestock) stand the imposing ruins of Frithelstock Priory, adjacent to the north-east side of the church. These are the only substantial remains of a former monastic house in Devon.

Returning to the Tarka Trail we follow the River Torridge to Annery Kiln, a former limekiln of the local Annery Estate, which used to produce lime fertiliser for the surrounding fields but now stands peacefully wrapped in ivy. We cross the river at Halfpenny Bridge, built in 1835 to connect the parishes of Monkleigh and Weare Giffard. This point is also the start of the tidal section of the River Torridge as it flows seaward towards the Bristol Channel.

We follow the quiet road through the pretty village of Weare Giffard before making our way along a series of footpaths through countryside and woodland to reach Huntshaw Wood. Hidden within the wood is Berry Castle, the remains of an Iron Age hill fort. A series of paths run through the wood, making it an enjoyable detour from our route.

The final section of our walk follows quiet lanes and footpaths through glorious countryside to return to Great Torrington.

GREAT TORRINGTON
DISTANCE: 21.5KM/13.4MILES » **TOTAL ASCENT:** 461M/1,512FT » **START GR:** : SS 480197 » **TIME:** ALLOW 6 HOURS » **SATNAV:** EX38 8JD » **MAP:** OS EXPLORER 126, CLOVELLY & HARTLAND, 1:25,000 » **REFRESHMENTS:** BLACK HORSE, TORRINGTON; CYDER PRESSE, WEARE GIFFARD » **NAVIGATION:** MAINLY STRAIGHTFORWARD ON PATHS AND LANES.

06 GREAT TORRINGTON

Directions – Great Torrington

↪ Join the Tarka trail at Great Torrington station and follow it south above the river until you reach the B3227. **Turn right** on to the road and follow it briefly before **turning right** again on to a footpath that heads uphill through woods and then across fields to a track. **Turn left** on to this and follow it past Priestacott. Continue past the road junction and then take the footpath **left** which follows the edges of fields generally north to reach a road.

2 **Turn right** on to the road and follow it towards Frithelstock, **turning left** on to a footpath just before entering the village (continue on the road into Frithelstock to visit the ruined priory). Follow this path across a large field and over a small stream through some trees, then cross another field to the next road. **Turn left** on to the road and follow it for a short distance before **turning right** on to another footpath heading north-east across fields to Monkleigh.

3 **Turn left** on to the road in Monkleigh and then take the first **right** – follow this road and **fork right** at the next junction. Follow the road downhill to reach a small car park just before the A386. Use the tunnel under the road to access the Tarka Trail; **turn left** on to it and follow it north to Annery Kiln.

4 **Turn right** off the Tarka Trail and on to the road, heading north-east past Annery Kiln and over Halfpenny Bridge. **Turn right** at the road junction and follow the road south towards Weare Giffard. **Turn left** on to a footpath just before you reach the church and follow this east, parallel to the road, across fields and through some woodland to reach a lane.

5 **Turn right** on to the lane and follow it downhill briefly until you can **turn left** on to another footpath heading east across more fields. The footpath curves to the left and crosses the lane to Southcott Barton before reaching another lane. **Turn right** on to this lane and then **left** through Cleave Farm, down a wooded lane to reach a road junction at Huntshaw Mill Bridge. **Keep right** here and follow the lane south, uphill and then downhill, towards Great Torrington.

6 At the road junction **turn right** and follow the road west and across the stream. Take the next footpath on the **left** which follows the course of the stream west and back to the start. (NB There are lots of different paths at different heights above the stream across this area of woodland which will bring you back to the start of the route or the Tarka Trail just north of the start.)

HALFPENNY BRIDGE

ROADFORD LAKE

07 **Roadford Lake**

21.4km/13.3miles

An exploration of Roadford Lake and nature reserve and the intriguing landscapes and settlements that surround it.

Headson car park » Breazle Farm » Eworthy » Witherdon Wood » Ivyhouse Cross » Westweek Barton » Germansweek » Roadford Lake bridge » Headson car park

Start

Roadford Lake Headson car park. GR: SX 439915.

The Walk

Our walk begins at Roadford Lake, a 730-acre reservoir set on the fringes of Dartmoor. A popular place for watersports, and the site of a six-metre sundial, there's an extensive network of trails and a campsite here should you wish to explore further. The lake is home to a wide variety of wildlife and important habitat, including species-rich Culm grassland. It is worth noting that the character of the land in this part of Devon means that it is often waterlogged and can be extremely wet underfoot after periods of rain.

From Roadford we follow clear bridleways across wide-open fields, crossing the River Wolf, the body of water which was impounded to create the lake in 1989. A gentle climb brings us to Eworthy and

Eworthy barrow at the very top of the hill, offering fine views back towards the lake and, further in the distance, the rolling uplands of Dartmoor.

We enter Witherdon Wood on wide forestry tracks. Much of the tree cover in this area is now coniferous but there are areas of broadleaf still remaining.

Emerging from the woods we follow quiet country lanes until a bridleway leads to open fields with further views across the lake. Crossing more fields brings us into the pretty village of Germansweek, with its Norman church and traditional cob and thatch cottages. From here we cross Roadford Lake at the nature reserve, thirty-four hectares of marshy grassland, dense scrub willow, broadleaved woodland and coniferous plantations – and home to a population of hazel dormice.

ROADFORD LAKE

DISTANCE: 21.4KM/13.3MILES » **TOTAL ASCENT:** 426M/1,398FT » **START GR:** SX 439915 » **TIME:** ALLOW 6 HOURS » **SATNAV:** EX20 4JR (NEAREST) » **MAP:** OS EXPLORER 112, LAUNCESTON & HOLSWORTHY, 1:25,000 » **REFRESHMENTS:** ROADFORD LAKE CAFE, SOUTHERN SHORE » **NAVIGATION:** EASY-TO-FOLLOW PATHS AND LANES.

FOOTBRIDGE FROM START ON TO LAKESIDE TRAIL

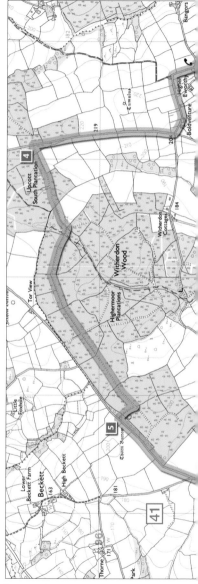

07 **ROADFORD LAKE**

Directions – Roadford Lake

⊙▸ Return to the road and **turn right**, heading south, to reach a **left turn** on to a signed bridleway. Follow this across fields into Breazle Farm. Continue on the track turning **left** in the farm and heading north out across fields. **Keep right** at the bridleway junction and follow the bridleway to a lane and then the road. **Turn left** on to the road and follow it for a short section to reach a signed footpath; **turn right** through the gate and across a field.

2 Follow the footpath across a field and through some woodland to reach a track. **Turn left** on to the track and cross the River Wolf and then **turn right** on to a footpath heading uphill across fields to reach the road at Eworthy.

3 **Turn right** on to the road and then **straight across** at Eworthy Cross heading north out of the village. Follow this road **left** around a sharp bend and then **turn right** at the next junction; follow this road north for about 1km to reach a **left turn** on to a forest track.

4 Follow the forest road west to a gate at a track junction; **turn right** here on to the main forest road which follows parallel to the northern edge of Witherdon Wood. **Ignore** the first right and follow the long very straight track to the next **right**; follow this to the road.

5 **Turn left** and follow the road to Ivyhouse Cross; **turn left** here and continue on the road for around 200m to a **left turn** on to a bridleway which starts down the farm track of Westweek Barton. Follow this to the end of the track and **trend left** downhill across a field to the woodland. Follow the bridleway across a stream and then **fork right** and uphill to reach the end of a track. **Turn right** on to this and follow it to the road.

6 **Turn left** on to the road and then **right** into Germansweek. Take the **right turn** in the village signed to the church and follow the footpath downhill across fields in a south-westerly direction above Southweek Wood. Drop down into the woodland and continue on the footpath above the lake to reach the road.

7 **Turn left** on to the road and cross the bridge over the north-eastern tip of Roadford Lake. Then take the **right turn** on to the bridleway and follow it parallel to the road and then around the land spit and back towards the road. **Turn right** on to the road and follow it back to the car park.

WITHERDON WOOD

08 **North Tawton** 28.3km/17.6miles

Follow the Tarka Trail and the Devonshire Heartland Way along the sparkling River Taw and through the rolling countryside of West Devon.

North Tawton » Bouchers Hill » Yeo » Tarka Trail » Bondleigh » Taw Green » Taw Bridge » Nymet Rowland » Blackditch Cross » Loosebeare » Gissage Lake » Devonshire Heartland Way » Ashridge Court » North Tawton

Start
Fore Street, North Tawton.
GR: SS 660017.

The Walk
The Devonshire Heartland Way runs for forty-three waymarked miles through the heart of Devon, linking the Exe Valley in the east with Okehampton on the edge of Dartmoor in the west. It takes in picturesque countryside, pretty villages, woodland and farmland. Our walk starts on the DHW, heading steeply up out of North Tawton. This small former market town was the long-term home of the poet Ted Hughes and is also where Taw Valley cheddar is made.

Our walk now joins the Tarka Trail, meandering along quiet country lanes with fine views over the surrounding countryside. Descending to the valley we follow the River Taw for several pleasant miles on its journey from the northern flanks of Dartmoor to the Bristol Channel at Bideford Bay.

In the spring and summer the riverbanks are ablaze with wild flowers – the daffodils in this part of the country are particularly dazzling in March and April – yellowhammers flit between the hedgerows and there are resident otters in the river.

Leaving the Tarka Trail, we head for Nymet Rowland, a small village that takes its name from 'Nymet', the old name for the nearby River Yeo. The station at Lapford is only a short walk from here, so the route could be joined at this point if arriving by train.

From Nymet Rowland we walk south, rejoining the DHW at Gissage Lake – actually a stream that runs eastwards to join the Yeo. Ascending to cross Ashridge Moor and then diving into a wooded river valley a final stretch of enjoyable walking returns us to Bouchers Hill and the descent back into North Tawton.

NORTH TAWTON
DISTANCE: 28.3KM/17.6MILES » **TOTAL ASCENT:** 531M/1,742FT » **START GR:** SS 660017 » **TIME:** ALLOW 8 HOURS » **SATNAV:** EX20 2DT » **MAP:** OS EXPLORER 113, OKEHAMPTON, 1:25,000 » **REFRESHMENTS:** KIRSTY'S KITCHEN, NORTH TAWTON » **NAVIGATION:** STRAIGHTFORWARD PATHS AND LANES.

CONT. ON PAGE 54

08 NORTH TAWTON

STARTS ON PAGE 52

CONT. ON PAGE 53

08 NORTH TAWTON

Directions – North Tawton

⊕ From Fore Street, walk north up the track following the Devonshire Heartland Way towards Bouchers Hill. **Turn right** at the gate and then **left** at the next corner following the path down a narrow track to reach a small bridge into a field. Follow the path uphill **trending left** across the next two fields to a path junction. **Continue** in the same direction and follow the path as it turns left and follows the stream downhill to the road at Yeo. **Turn right** on the road and follow it across the bridge to join the Tarka Trail.

2 **Turn right** on to the Tarka Trail heading north across fields and following the River Taw. Join a track which becomes a road and **turn right** at the junction, following the road to Bondleigh. **Turn left** on to the road and then **almost immediately right** on to a footpath following the river. Where the path rejoins the road, **turn right** and follow the road north (there is a short section of beautiful river path you can follow if you turn right after the second house; it rejoins the road through a gate). Continue on the road **turning right** at Taw Green and then **right** on to the B3220. Follow this road for a short distance to reach a footpath **left** just after the bridge.

3 Follow this path north-east across several fields, following the path of the river to the corner of a wood. Follow the path along the edge of the wood to reach a road. Cross the road and take the bridleway opposite into the next field, following this roughly east across the fields to the south of the small barn and across the next field to the road. Cross the road and follow the path through the field to the north of the farm before **trending right** slightly downhill to reach a small area of woodland and a gate. **Continue** on the path downhill through this into the next field. Cross the next large field heading north-east to reach the road.

4 **Turn right** on to the road and follow it across a stream and uphill into Nymet Rowland. Follow the road through the village and then downhill heading south-east. Take the next **right** and follow the road down to the junction with the B3220 at Blackditch Cross. Cross here and follow Blackditch Lane uphill to a **left turn** on to a rough track called Loosebeare Lane.

5 Follow Loosebeare Lane to some farm buildings and then **turn right** and follow the larger road through the farm with most of the buildings on your left. Continue on this lane heading south past a large house on the left and then out across fields. The track takes a sharp right then left and then heads downhill to a footbridge above Gissage Lake; cross this bridge to reach a road.

6 Cross the road and take the footpath opposite, climbing through woodland to reach a field. Follow the footpath up the hill and then **turn right** following the hedge and footpath signs across the field and over a small bridge into the next field. Here you rejoin the Devonshire Heartland Way (DHW) and follow it back to the start. Cross the next few fields keeping high until the last one where you drop down through a gate and over a footbridge (**don't** cross the bridge made of an old trailer in the previous field!). Head slightly **right** and uphill across the next field to reach a gate on to a lane.

7 **Turn left** on to the lane and follow it for about 50m to a **right turn** on to a footpath heading generally west across fields to reach the next road south of Lower Newton. **Turn left** on to the road and then **right** at the next junction. Follow the road slightly uphill and take the **left** at Newton Cross. Follow this road to reach Ashridge Moor Cross. **Continue straight over** and head west on Ashridge Lane towards Ashridge Court. Follow the bridleway and the DHW on lanes past some buildings trending **left** to head south past High Ridge Farm and down a road towards North Tawton. Take the next **left** on to North Street and follow this to the square, **turning right** here on to Fore Street to return to the start of the walk.

FOOTPATH UP BOUCHERS HILL

SECTION 3

Mid & East Devon

Mid Devon covers the area between Devon's two national parks, Dartmoor and Exmoor. Scored through by the Exe Valley, the walking here takes in rolling hills, picturesque villages, deciduous woodland and country estates.

East Devon is packed with fascinating features. The South West Cost Path follows the fossil-strewn Jurassic Coast World Heritage Site from the sandy seaside town of Exmouth east into Dorset. Walking here takes in wild coastal headlands, pebble beaches and intriguing rock formations. Further inland lie the rare pebblebed heathlands and hill fort at Woodbury, ripe for exploration.

VIEW WEST FROM BEER HEAD (ROUTE 12)

WELLINGTON MONUMENT

09 Culm Valley & the Blackdown Hills 16km/9.9miles

An intriguing tour of the Blackdown Hills, visiting the Culm Valley and the Wellington Monument, with plenty of opportunities to take in the views.

Culmstock » Bowhayes Farm » Hackpen Hill » Tedburrow Farm » Whitehall » Pen Cross » Wellington Monument » Black Down Common » Culmstock Beacon » Pitt Farm » Culmstock

Start
Culmstock village. GR: ST 102135.

The Walk

The River Culm is the longest tributary of the River Exe, carving its way east to west from Culmhead in Somerset to join the River Exe at Exeter. Our walk begins in Culmstock, deep in the Culm Valley and on the edge of the Blackdown Hills, a 143-square-mile Area of Outstanding Natural Beauty that straddles the Devon/Somerset border. Reaching a high point of 315 metres at Staple Hill, the Blackdown plateau is dotted with historical fortifications, dating from the Iron Age to the Second World War. The area is also home to some sixteen Sites of Special Scientific Interest.

Leaving Culmstock we climb the wooded flanks of Hackpen Hill, taking in views across the Culm Valley before descending back to the river. We make our way enjoyably along peaceful lanes and footpaths, weaving through the countryside and along the western ridge of shapely Combe Hill.

Take in the views after the initial ascent before you disappear into the woods.

From Combe Hill we sneak across the border into Somerset to ascend the distinctive circular hill on top of which stands the Wellington Monument. Emerging from the beech trees this fifty-three-metre structure is an imposing site; owned by the National Trust it is the tallest three-sided obelisk in the world. Take a moment to enjoy far-reaching views out to Exmoor on a clear day and spot the artwork by local street artist, Banksy.

Returning to Devon we head across Black Down Common to reach Culmstock Beacon, a fascinating place to explore the stone roundhouse and trig point, or pause for a moment on the thoughtfully positioned carved wooden bench. This was one of a number of Elizabethan beacons built to warn of approaching ships. From the beacon a steep descent brings us back to the River Culm and we follow this to return to Culmstock.

CULM VALLEY & THE BLACKDOWN HILLS

DISTANCE: 16KM/9.9MILES **» TOTAL ASCENT:** 389M/1,276FT **» START GR:** ST 102135 **» TIME:** ALLOW 4.5 HOURS **» SATNAV:** EX15 3JD **» MAP:** OS EXPLORER 128, TAUNTON & BLACKDOWN HILLS, 1:25,000 **» REFRESHMENTS:** CULM VALLEY INN, CULMSTOCK **» NAVIGATION:** GOOD PATHS AND LANES ARE EASY TO FOLLOW.

BLACKDOWN COMMON

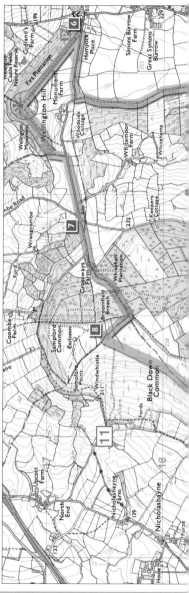

09 CULM VALLEY & THE BLACKDOWN HILLS

Directions – Culm Valley & the Blackdown Hills

❺► Follow the main road east to the end of the houses where you can **turn right** over a stile and on to a footpath. Follow the path uphill, trending slightly **left** across a series of fields and stiles to reach a lane.

2 **Turn left** on to the lane and then **right** on to the path which goes through Bowhayes Farm, exiting at the top **left** of the yard and then crossing a small field to a stile in the top **left** corner. **Turn left** here and follow a track towards a house. **Turn right** on to a footpath and head uphill into some woods. Take the **left–hand fork** and continue uphill through woodland, emerging on to Hackpen Hill on the ridge above. Follow the path north-east along the ridge until you reach a lane.

3 **Turn left** and follow the lane downhill through Tedburrow Farm until you reach the junction with the B3391. Cross this road and follow the footpath across the fields heading north-west to some buildings. **Continue** on the path as it heads north across a series of fields and small footbridges to reach the road at Whitehall.

4 **Turn right** on to the road and then take the **left turn** following the road uphill. Take the **first right** and continue on the road until you can take an obvious wide path **right** heading slightly downhill. Follow this path past a couple of fields and across a small bridge, then **trend left** and uphill across a field to reach a lane.

5 **Turn left** on to the lane and follow it uphill, **forking left** and continuing uphill to the sharp right turn at the top. Continue **straight ahead** on to the path here and follow it along the edge of some woods and across a small field. **Continue** on the path heading north to reach a road. **Turn right** on to the road and follow it until you can **turn left** into the National Trust Wellington Monument car park.

6 Follow the main track through the car park and head north-west through the woods to the Wellington Monument. Continue past this and on to a smaller path heading south-west along the edge of some woodland. Follow this path (signed as a National Trust circular walk) along the edge of the wood and then curving downhill to the right where you reach a gate. Go through the gate and **turn left** on to a bridleway; follow this to the road. Cross the road and **turn right**, following it to the junction where the road turns sharply right.

7 Leave the main road and continue south-west on a bridleway (initially a lane) uphill past Crossways Farm buildings, **forking right** through a large gate into some woods. Continue uphill on the track passing the phone mast on the left to reach another gate on to Black Down Common. **Turn right** here and follow a smaller path north-west until you reach a pond.

8 **Turn left** at the pond and join a wide, grassy fire break heading south-west across the common. Follow this until you reach the rocky track again. Follow the track, heading for the western tip of the woods and another pond. **Turn left** uphill just after the pond and then **trend right** on to the open common ground. Follow the paths south to reach the trig point, bench and stone hut at Culmstock Beacon.

9 Drop down the steep path by the bench to reach a track. **Turn left** on to the track and follow it, turning **right** and heading downhill on a roughly surfaced lane past an electricity building. Go through a gate at the bottom of this and follow the road **left** signed to Pitt Farm.

10 **Turn right** on to a signed footpath just before the farm buildings and then go through an old metal gate. Follow the path to the bottom **left** of the field and find the stile in the hedge just before the gate into the next field. Follow the path across the next field heading **right** to the gate near the house. **Turn right** on to the road and follow it for a short section until you can **turn left** on to a footpath. Follow the path around the house and across a field to a small footbridge. Cross the bridge and **turn right**; the path follows the course of the river across fields and then into Culmstock, emerging near the church. **Turn left** here and head uphill to reach the main road and the end of the walk.

ASHCLYST FOREST

10 Killerton Estate & Ashclyst Forest   14.1km/8.8miles

A tour of the 6,400-acre Killerton Estate, taking in a working watermill, an extinct volcano, an eighteenth-century mansion and a butterfly-filled forest.

Broadclyst » M5 crossing » Killerton House » Killerton Park » Budlake » Sprydon Plantation » Ashclyst Forest » Clyst Valley » New Inn » Broadclyst

Start

Broadclyst, near the church and the Red Lion pub. GR: SX 982972.

The Walk

Nestled at the heart of the 6,400-acre Killerton Estate, the pretty village of Broadclyst was once divided by the A38, the major route to the West Country. Now bypassed by the M5 motorway, the village is once again a pleasant place to explore. The working watermill at Clyston Mill supplies flour locally and is fascinating to visit – check opening times before you arrive.

From Broadclyst our walk heads for majestic Killerton Park, crossing the thundering motorway before escaping back into tranquil countryside. The estate is National Trust owned and the eighteenth-century house, former residence of the Acland family, sits within landscaped gardens and parkland. The house and gardens are paid/NT-member entry, however the park is open to the public. We begin our tour of the grounds passing the house itself before heading out to explore the park. The monument near Bluebell Gate was erected in 1873 to the memory of Sir Thomas Dyke Acland. Further into the estate we climb the Iron Age hill fort and extinct volcano at Dolbury Hill for wonderful views out over the Exe Estuary.

Leaving Killerton behind we again cross the M5, this time to reach the leafy surroundings of Ashclyst Forest. This area was once mixed land with fields, wood and heathland until it was planted with conifers during the nineteenth century to provide timber for the Killerton Estate. The resulting 300-hectare woodland is now one of the largest in East Devon, with a number of waymarked trails and an abundance of wildlife. Butterflies are a speciality here, including very rare pearl-bordered fritillaries in spring and white admirals in summer.

Finally, crossing the River Clyst, which runs along the Clyst Valley to the Exe Estuary, we follow quiet lanes to return to Broadclyst.

KILLERTON ESTATE & ASHCLYST FOREST

DISTANCE: 14.1KM/8.8MILES » **TOTAL ASCENT:** 245M/804FT » **START GR:** SX 982972 » **TIME:** ALLOW 4.5 HOURS » **SATNAV:** EX5 3EL » **MAP:** OS EXPLORER 114, EXETER & THE EXE VALLEY, AND A SMALL SECTION OF OS EXPLORER 115, EXMOUTH & SIDMOUTH, BOTH 1:25,000 » **REFRESHMENTS:** RED LION, BROADCLYST; CAFE AND RESTAURANT AT KILLERTON » **NAVIGATION:** CLEAR AND EASY-TO-FOLLOW PATHS AND LANES EXCEPT IN ASHCLYST FOREST WHERE THE CORRECT PATH CHOICE CAN BE CONFUSING BUT DOESN'T REALLY MATTER.

ASHCLYST FOREST

10 KILLERTON ESTATE & ASHCLYST FOREST

Directions – Killerton Estate & Ashclyst Forest

⮕ Follow Church Close north behind the Red Lion pub and join the footpath at the end. Follow this downhill into a small wood and across the footbridge, then cross a field to reach a track. This is the Killerton–Broadclyst family cycle track (KBFCT). **Turn right** on to this and follow it through Martinsfields Farm to a track junction. Take the **left fork**, leaving the KBFCT, and follow a footpath heading north across more fields. Follow the path over the motorway bridge to reach the end of a lane at Francis Court Farm.

2 Follow the lane and **turn right** on to a larger road. Follow this for 200m before **turning left** through a gate next to the drive into the National Trust Killerton Estate. Follow the footpath across the parkland to the south of the house and gardens to reach a path junction in the south-west corner of the gardens. **Turn right** here and follow the path north, uphill, along the edge of the gardens passing the monument about halfway up. Near the top of this path, and close to a well-positioned bench, is Bluebell Gate; **turn right** through this.

3 Follow the path **right** and through another gate, continuing on the path as it curves towards a bench and then taking the **right-hand fork**. **Continue straight on** through a path junction and around the southern side of the Iron Age hill fort on Dolbury Hill. Now follow the path trending east downhill but **turning left** to avoid entering the paid-entry NT gardens. **Turn right** and follow the large track downhill to the road.

4 **Turn right** on to the road and follow it for 400m before **turning left** on to a path that heads east across some fields and under the motorway. Follow this path to reach the lane through Budlake to reach the B3181.

5 Cross the road and follow the lane east past Budlake House towards Ashclyst Forest. Once the lane enters the forest take the **second right** following a forest road into the wood. Take the next **left** on another forest track and follow this to reach the road again at a T-junction. Cross the road and follow the minor road east for a short section until you can **turn right** on to a track.

6 Follow this track south, **turning left** at the next junction and following this east taking the next **left** and then **right** on to a lane. Follow the lane east and then **right** on to a path heading south near the edge of the forest. Continue on this trail following the edge of the forest south with a couple of detours into and back out of the woods. Take the **left** turn to reach the south-east corner of Ashclyst Forest where you leave the woods and head across a field to reach a road by Ashclyst Cottages.

7 **Turn right** on to the road and follow it south-west towards Broadclyst. Take the footpath opposite the New Inn across fields and back into the village. Take a **right** on the road you reach and then **left** at the end of the road to return to the start of the walk.

KILLERTON HOUSE

WOODBURY COMMON & OTTERTON

DISTANCE: 23.5KM/14.6MILES » **TOTAL ASCENT:** 514M/1,686FT » **START GR:** SY 041881 » **TIME:** ALLOW 7 HOURS »
SATNAV: EX5 1EZ » **MAP:** OS EXPLORER 115, EXMOUTH & SIDMOUTH, 1:25,000 » **REFRESHMENTS:** THE SIR WALTER
RALEIGH, EAST BUDLEIGH » **NAVIGATION:** EASY-TO-FOLLOW PATHS AND LANES. SEVERAL PATH OPTIONS ON SECTIONS OF
COMMON BUT STRAIGHTFORWARD NAVIGATION.

WOODLAND DESCENDING TO LADRAM BAY

11 Woodbury Common & Otterton · 23.5km/14.6miles

Cross East Devon's rare pebblebed heathland on a journey through time to discover an Iron Age hill fort and a coastline that dates back 185 million years.

The Warren car park » Woodbury Castle » Woodbury Common » Bicton Common » East Budleigh Common » East Budleigh » Clamour Bridge » Crab Ledge on the SWCP » Ladram Bay » High Peak » Tortoiseshell Rocks » Pinn » B3178 » Colaton Raleigh Common » The Warren car park

Start

The Warren car park, Woodbury.
GR: SY 041881.

The Walk

Woodbury Common is an area of heathland comprising the commons of Lympstone, East Budleigh, Shortwood, Dalditch, Bicton, Colaton Raleigh and Woodbury. The commons are underlaid by rare pebblebeds, dating from the Triassic era. Lying within the East Devon Area of Outstanding Natural Beauty it's a fascinating place to explore, with particular points of interest including the prehistoric earthworks at Woodbury Castle, and Hayes Barton, birthplace of Sir Walter Raleigh.

Our walk begins at the highest point on the commons, The Warren, at 176 metres, from where there are fine views out across the heathlands to the coast. From here we head to Woodbury Castle, constructed between 500–300 BC but possibly used again between 1798 and 1803 during the Napoleonic wars. The wooded ditches and ramparts make for an enjoyable exploration. Continuing on the East Devon Way, a thirty-eight-mile waymarked trail that links Exmouth with Lyme Regis, we cross the commons to reach the River Otter. This is the area of England's first licensed beaver reintroduction and monitoring programme.

Our next stop is the South West Coast Path along a fascinating stretch of the Jurassic Coast. The exposed rocks along this part of the coast provide a continuous sequence of Triassic, Jurassic and Cretaceous rock formations spanning approximately 185 million years of the Earth's history. Ladram Bay, away from its vast holiday park, is home to a number of incredible red sandstone sea stacks which rise like sculptures from the sea. Further along, steep climbs up High Peak and Peak Hill are rewarded with great views of the countryside and interesting coastline. Heading inland again we make a second crossing of the River Otter and climb back on to the commons, rejoining the East Devon Way to finish.

NOTE: This walk passes close to a military firing range on Colaton Raleigh Common. Check the MOD's online Straightpoint and Woodbury Common Training Area Grenade Range's firing times and do not enter the area when red flags are flying.

CONT. ON PAGE 78 ▶

11 WOODBURY COMMON & OTTERTON

CONT. ON PAGE 77

STARTS ON PAGE 76

VIEW NORTH FROM HIGH PEAK

Directions – Woodbury Common & Otterton

 Leave the car park and head south-west along the path which follows the course of the road but stays a short distance from it. Cross the East Devon Way and continue on the track as it curves left and heads south towards the wooded area around Woodbury Castle. Follow the track **left** around the edge of the woodland (or cut through and explore the castle) to the most southern point of woodland, then follow the track south to reach and cross the road near to Four Firs car park.

2 **Fork right** after crossing the road and follow the track to rejoin the EDW. **Turn left** and follow it through a small wooded area and along tracks to the east of the quarry lakes marked on the map. Continue south on the EDW crossing a road on to East Budleigh Common. Take the first path **left** and follow it south-east to reach another lane and car park on Hayeswood Lane.

3 Follow the path along Hayeswood Lane through Hayes Wood to reach a fork in the byway; take the **left fork** and follow it into East Budleigh. **Turn right** on to Middle Street and follow this on to Lower Budleigh road. Cross the B3178 and continue on Frogmore Road. Follow this for 200m and then **turn right** on to the farm track and then footpath through Thorn Mill Farm and past the water works. Follow the path across some fields to a path junction, **turning left** and then crossing the River Otter on Clamour Bridge.

4 **Turn right** and follow the byway east through some trees and across fields to reach a road. **Turn right** and follow the road south to a track junction. **Turn left** here and follow Stantyway Road north-east for a short distance. Take the **first right** and follow the track and then footpath towards the sea at Crab Ledge. **Turn left** on to the South West Coast path (SWCP) and follow it north above Ladram Bay and past High Peak, optionally climbing the steps to the top for views along the coast.

5 Continue north-east along the SWCP for another kilometre, then take the next footpath **left**, leaving the SWCP above Tortoiseshell Rocks. Follow this path along the edge of some woodland to reach a road. **Turn left** on to the road and follow it uphill and through Pinn to a road junction. **Turn right** here and follow the road to Burnthouse Farm.

6 Take the footpath **left** just after the house, signed *Colaton Raleigh*. Follow it west across some fields and over the River Otter to reach a road called Eden Way on the east side of Colaton Raleigh. Follow the road west for a short distance and then **turn right** up a track. Follow this north and then around the left-hand bend to reach the road. **Turn right** on to the road and follow this to the junction with the B3178.

7 **Turn right** and follow the main road for about 100m then **turn left** on to Naps Lane. Follow this west for about 2km to reach a road junction. **Turn right** on to the road and then **left** on to the EDW heading south-west across Colaton Raleigh Common. After about 2km on the EDW take the third main **right** on a track back to the start.

WOODBURY COMMON

WEST CLIFF FROM BRANSCOMBE BEACH

12 Branscombe

A tour of the deep combes and high clifftop trails around the picturesque historical village of Branscombe.

Branscombe Beach » Beer Head » Beer » Seaton Hole » Beer Caves » Branscombe Beach » Weston Cliff » Weston Mouth » Donkey Sanctuary » Edge Farm » Edge Barton » Branscombe » Branscombe Beach

Start

Branscombe seafront car park.
GR: SY 207881.

The Walk

Nestled at the meeting place of several steep combes, Branscombe – claimed to be the longest village in the country – is a delightful place to explore. Cob and thatch cottages adorned with flowers line the narrow lanes, all of which lead to the sea at Branscombe Mouth. From here the wide pebble beach and soaring headland make for inviting and intriguing walking.

Our route begins at the beach and heads up the wide grassy slopes of East Cliff. The views from Beer Head at the top are well worth the climb – keep a look out for dolphins and porpoises playing in the waves below. Following the South West Coast Path we descend towards Beer with continuous views along the Jurassic Coast. This ninety-five-mile stretch between East Devon and West Dorset is a UNESCO World Heritage Site. The area's geology displays some 185 million years of the Earth's history and is considered one of the most important sites in the world for geological research and teaching.

Our walk now descends to Beer, a pretty village and former smugglers' cove. Beer Quarry Caves are open for exploration in the summer months (paid entry) – the Beer Stone taken from here was used to build twenty-four cathedrals across Britain.

Back at Branscombe, we now set off on the western loop of the walk, following the South West Coast Path out of the village up West Cliff. From here there is glorious coastal walking, passing the Iron Age hill fort at Berry Cliff Camp and the trig point at Weston Cliff. Heading inland up the deep, tree-lined Weston Combe we return to the village past the National Trust's Manor Mill, the Old Bakery tearoom and the working forge.

BRANSCOMBE

DISTANCE: 21KM/13MILES » **TOTAL ASCENT:** 693M/2,274FT » **START GR:** SY 207881 » **TIME:** ALLOW 6 HOURS » **SATNAV:** EX12 3DP » **MAP:** OS EXPLORER 115, EXMOUTH & SIDMOUTH, AND A SMALL SECTION ON OS EXPLORER 116, LYME REGIS & BRIDPORT, BOTH 1:25,000 » **REFRESHMENTS:** THE MASONS ARMS OR THE FOUNTAIN HEAD PUBS, BRANSCOMBE » **NAVIGATION:** EASY-TO-FOLLOW COAST PATH, INLAND PATHS AND LANES.

12 BRANSCOMBE

Directions – Branscombe

5 Cross the road at the entrance to the car park and **turn left** (while facing the sea), go through the gate and head east up the long grassy hill of East Cliff. Cross a stile at the top of the first field and continue uphill and up steep steps in an easterly direction. **Keep right** where the path forks, walking around the edge of the fields to join the South West Coast Path at Beer Head. Continue on the SWCP, now heading north-east past a campsite and then join a road which drops down into Beer.

2 Stay on the SWCP (signed *Seaton*) and follow the path up zigzagging steps out of Beer to reach a lane near Seaton Hole. **Turn left** on to the lane and leave the SWCP. Head south-west uphill on the lane and join New Road (B3174). **Turn left** on to the road but use the permissive bridleway which follows it, rejoining the road for a short section at the end of the path then taking the **left turn** on to Long Hill. Follow this road downhill and around a left-hand bend to reach the main street with the village shop on your left. **Turn right** on to this road and follow it west, signed to Beer Caves. The road joins the National Cycle Network Route 2 as it continues on to Quarry Lane. Follow this uphill past the entrance to Beer Quarry Caves then **turn left** on to a footpath signed *Vicarage*.

3 Follow the path through some woodland and then across some fields to reach a stile. Follow the path downhill through woodland **staying left** at the obvious path junction until you reach a road. **Turn left** on to the road and follow it for a short section before **turning right** on to a private road to *Little Seaside* which is also signed *Public Footpath*. Follow this downhill towards the house and then follow the footpath which goes through the field to the **left** of the house, joining the main path behind the house. **Turn left** on to this path to return to Branscombe Mouth.

4 The second loop heads out from Branscombe on the SWCP in a westerly direction. Start following the path uphill past the Sea Shanty cafe and slightly inland around the house. The path then forks; take the **left fork** on to the SWCP and head uphill into some woods and up steps along the clifftop. Follow the path as it drops down to the right, away from the cliff edge through some woodland. Continue to follow SWCP signs to Weston Mouth. Follow the track **turning left** into a small quarry, then **right** uphill and into some fields. Follow the edge of fields until you **turn left** down steps and across another field to reach the beach at Weston Mouth.

5   Cross the stream here and then **turn right**, leaving the SWCP and heading north on a footpath up the wooded valley to reach the road by the Donkey Sanctuary. **Turn left** on to the lane and then **right** on to the main road heading east. Follow it for about 1km to where you can **turn left** at Ashton Farm.

6   Follow the footpath north-east past some farm buildings to the end of the track and across some fields to reach another lane. Cross the lane and follow the minor road, marked as a dead end, towards Edge Farm. Follow the track to the farm, taking the **first right** and heading south-east towards Edge Barton. Join the footpath at the end of the track and continue in the same direction down the valley, reaching a small road near Hole House.

7   **Turn right** and follow the road uphill before **turning left** on to a footpath into a field. The path follows the top edge of the field and then drops down and crosses the stream on a sleeper bridge. Cross the stream then **turn right**, following the path contouring along the fields below a house, through a gate and then up to the road. **Turn right** on to the road and follow it downhill to a road junction. Cross the road and **turn left then right** on to a small lane signed *Footpath to Branscombe Mouth*. Follow the lane to the end where you join a footpath heading in the same direction. Follow this trending **right** to return to Branscombe Mouth.

VIEW WEST FROM EAST CLIFF

SECTION 4

Dartmoor

Dartmoor covers 368 square miles of southern Devon, a diverse and varied landscape punctuated by granite tors and the relics of millennia of human habitation. The walks in this section take in some of the highlights of the national park, including High Willhays – the summit of southern England; Fingle Bridge, in a deep river valley below the imposing structure of Castle Drogo; and the Dewerstone with its eerie local legends. They visit high, windswept moors, ancient sessile oak woodland and some of the many fascinating historical sites on the moor, dotted with stone circles and abandoned ruins.

LOOKING WEST DOWN THE FOOTPATH WITH CASTLE DROGO TO THE RIGHT (ROUTE 14)

BRAT TOR – HIGH WILLHAYS

DISTANCE: 21.7KM/13.5MILES » **TOTAL ASCENT:** 971M/3,186FT » **START GR:** SX 525853 » **TIME:** ALLOW 7 HOURS »
SATNAV: EX20 4AY » **MAP:** OS EXPLORER OL28, DARTMOOR, 1:25,000, AND HARVEY SUPERWALKER DARTMOOR NORTH,
1:25,000 » **REFRESHMENTS:** THE DARTMOOR INN, LYDFORD » **NAVIGATION:** IN POOR VISIBILITY, YOU WILL NEED TO BE
PROFICIENT AT WALKING ON A BEARING TO SAFELY COMPLETE THIS WALK. IF IN DOUBT, THE LOOP FROM KITTY TOR, OVER
HIGH WILLHAYS AND BACK TO KITTY TOR COULD BE OMITTED AS THIS SECTION CROSSES AREAS OF HIGH MOORLAND ON
VAGUE PATHS.

FOOTPATH ABOVE MELDON RESERVOIR

13 Brat Tor – High Willhays

A tour of the north-west corner of Dartmoor, taking in wild and windswept moorland, soaring ridgelines and High Willhays, the summit of southern England.

Car park » Widgery Cross » Great Links Tor » Kitty Tor » Lyd Head » Branscombe's Loaf » West Okement River crossing » Yes Tor » High Willhays » Dinger Tor » Lints Tor » Kitty Tor » Green Tor » Rattle Brook » Car park

Start

Car park at the end of the lane behind the Dartmoor Inn. GR: SX 525853.

The Walk

From our start in the village of Lydford we head to Brat Tor, on the western edge of Dartmoor, easily distinguishable by the towering granite monument of Widgery Cross which stands on its summit. Placed there in 1887 to commemorate Queen Victoria's Golden Jubilee, it is visible from miles around, and therefore a good way-marker for the first section of our walk.

Our next stop is Great Links Tor, which stands in a commanding position overlooking Doetor Common and Nattor Down. One of the tor's granite stacks is twelve metres high, making this one of the highest points on Dartmoor. Taking in some of the best of this wild and windswept part of the moor we climb to Kitty Tor before walking along the inviting line of Corn Ridge. The River Lyd rises here at Lyd Head, flowing off the moor and through Lydford Gorge – the deepest gorge in south-west England – before joining the River Tamar. The gorge is

worth a visit for its impressive rocky landscape, boiling whirlpools and the thirty-metre-high White Lady waterfall (National Trust members/paid entry).

Dropping down from the ridge we reach the West Okement River. Just upstream from our crossing point stands Black-a-Tor Copse or Black Tor Beare, one of the finest examples of high-altitude oak woodland in Britain and the remnants of the trees that would once have covered Dartmoor. We now climb steeply to the summit of Dartmoor and the airy ridge on which stand Yes Tor and High Willhays. At 621 metres above sea level this is the highest point in England south of the Peak District. Leaving High Willhays we descend enjoyably back to the West Okement River, crossing sweeping open moorland to return to Lydford.

NOTE: This walk crosses a military range. Please check the firing times for WILLSWORTHY RANGE before undertaking this walk and do not enter the area when red flags are flying.

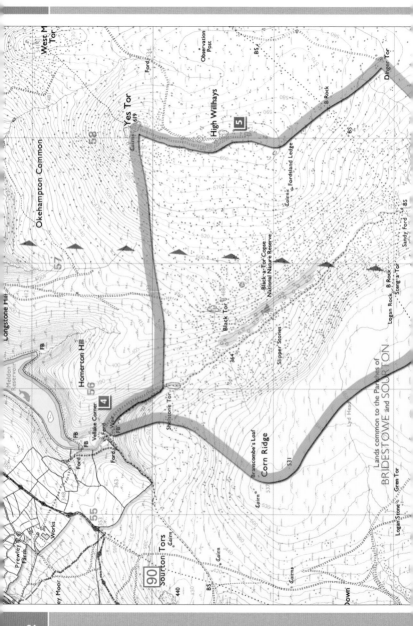

West M_ Tor

Observation Post

BS

Dinger Tor

Yes Tor
619

High Willhays

5

B Rock

Okehampton Common

Cairns

Cairns ← Fordsland Ledge

BS

Longstone Hill

Black-a-Tor Copse
National Nature Reserve

Sandy Ford

BS

Melden_ Reservoir

FB

Homerton Hill

Black Tor

Logan Rock   B Rock

FB

364

Slipper Stones

Stenga Tor

Veltake Corner
Ford

FB

4

Shelstone Tor

FB

Branscombe's Loaf

Lands common to the Parishes of
BRIDESTOWE and SOURTON

Prewley Farm

Works

Ford

Ford

Corn Ridge

Lyd Head

Gren Tor

Logan Stone

531

Cairns

Sourton
Tors

Cairns

Cairns

90

Cairns

BS

Logan Stone

Down

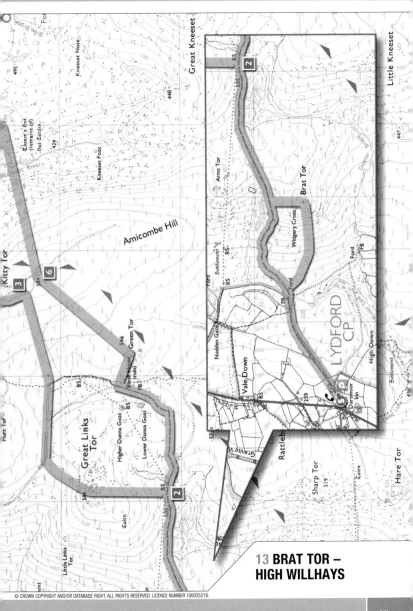

13 BRAT TOR – HIGH WILLHAYS

Directions – Brat Tor – High Willhays

➎ From the car park follow the main path north-east slightly uphill towards the obvious summit of Brat Tor and Widgery Cross. Dip down and cross the young River Lyd on stepping stones and then take the **right-hand fork**, climbing steeply and aiming directly for the rocky summit. From the summit head north following vague paths to reach the main bridleway. **Turn right** here and follow the bridleway east.

2 After about 1km **turn left** and leave the main path, heading uphill to Great Links Tor. Drop off the other side of the tor and head north-east to reach another track; **turn right** here and follow the track to Kitty Tor.

3 **Turn left** at Kitty Tor and head north-west following a track initially and then making your own way along the ridge passing Lyd Head and the rocks at Branscombe's Loaf. From here **turn right** and head north-east downhill to Shelstone Tor, then north to the weir and small bridge across the West Okement River (or follow the river further downstream to a larger bridge).

4 Once you have crossed the river, **turn right** and take the track uphill following the river in the direction of Black Tor. When the path peters out **turn left** and make your way uphill across open moor to the flag-poled and rocky summit of Yes Tor. **Turn right** and follow the summit ridge path south to High Willhays.

5 From High Willhays descend south-east to Dinger Tor (aim left of the tor if the visibility is bad to hit the track). **Turn right** after Dinger Tor and head south-west to Lints Tor. Continue west through the steep valley and up to Kitty Tor.

6 From Kitty Tor cross the moor to Green Tor and then drop down to the bridleway in Rattle Brook, or follow the track west and then take the bridleway **left**, heading south down Rattle Brook. Follow this path as it turns to the right and heads back past Great Links Tor and to the north of Brat Tor, continuing downhill across the stepping stones and back to the car park.

STEPPING STONES OVER THE RIVER LYD

PATH BETWEEN CASTLE DROGO AND FINGLE BRIDGE

14 **Fingle Bridge, Castle Drogo & the Teign Gorge** 16km/9.9miles

Meander through tranquil woodland alongside the River Teign before climbing up the steep valley to Castle Drogo for breathtaking views of Dartmoor.

Chagford » Chagford Bridge » Rushford Mill » Hunter's Tor » Castle Drogo » Piddledown Common » Rectory Wood » Fingle Bridge » Hannicombe Wood » Whiddon Wood » Chagford

Start

Chagford long-stay car park, Stableyard, Chagford TQ13 8DP. GR: SX 701874.

The Walk

From the pretty town of Chagford we descend to the River Teign, crossing at Chagford Bridge, a sixteenth–seventeenth-century grade II-listed granite structure. Immediately after the bridge a footpath leads us along the north bank of the river and into the gradually deepening gorge of the Teign valley.

Continuing along the north bank – also known as the Fisherman's Path – we ascend the side of the valley on the Hunter's Path, passing the craggy outcrop of Hunter's Tor to reach the wonderfully named Piddledown Common. Above this broods the great, grey, granite Castle Drogo, recently revealed after several years under scaffolding. This grade I-listed castle was built between 1911 and 1939 for Julius Drewe, businessman and founder of the Home and Colonial Stores, to designs by architect Edwin Lutyens. Despite

being the last castle built in England it has suffered badly from water damage, predominantly due to its medieval-style flat roof construction. A five-year restoration project by the National Trust has made the castle watertight for the first time in its history. Entry to Drogo is paid for non-National Trust members, however the gardens and cafe are open to the public.

From Drogo a long, winding descent through woodland brings us to the stunning setting of Fingle Bridge, a seventeenth-century packhorse bridge over a wide, shallow section of the River Teign. The bridge is named after the Fingle Brook, which flows into the Teign adjacent to the bridge. Fingle Woods are currently being restored through a combined project by the National Trust and the Woodland Trust. The whole valley is a haven for wildlife, including dippers, kingfishers and herons on the water; mewling buzzards circling high above the trees; red wood ants; deer and several species of the fritillary butterfly.

FINGLE BRIDGE, CASTLE DROGO & THE TEIGN GORGE

DISTANCE: 16KM/9.9MILES » **TOTAL ASCENT:** 380M/1,247FT » **START GR:** SX 701874 » **TIME:** ALLOW 5 HOURS » **SATNAV:** TQ13 8DP » **MAP:** OS EXPLORER OL28, DARTMOOR, 1:25,000 AND HARVEY SUPERWALKER, DARTMOOR NORTH, 1:25,000 » **REFRESHMENTS:** NATIONAL TRUST CAFE AT CASTLE DROGO; FINGLE BRIDGE INN » **NAVIGATION:** CLEAR, WELL-MARKED PATHS.

14 FINGLE BRIDGE, CASTLE DROGO & THE TEIGN GORGE

Directions – Fingle Bridge, Castle Drogo & the Teign Gorge

➎ From the car park head past the church into central Chagford, then continue (north-west) down Mill Street to reach a crossroads known as Factory Cross. **Turn right** here and follow the lane over a small stream to the packhorse bridge (Chagford Bridge). Cross the bridge and immediately afterwards **turn right** on to the footpath along the north bank of the River Teign.

2 Follow the footpath along the river to the next road. **Turn left** on the road and follow it until you can **turn right** on to a footpath just beyond Chagford swimming pool. Follow the footpath along the river. **Carefully** cross the A382 and continue following the river to a gate into a wood.

3 **Turn left** here and follow the path uphill signed *Castle Drogo*. At the top of the hill after a cattle grid take a **sharp right**, again following a path signed *Castle Drogo*. Follow this path around a **left-hand turn** and then contour along the top of the valley below the castle. **Turn left** at a set of steps to detour to the castle and National Trust cafe, or alternatively continue onwards.

4 Follow the high path signed towards Fingle Bridge. **Turn left** uphill through a gate and across some fields into Rectory Wood. **Turn right** at the path junction and follow the bridleway around the hill and then downhill in a south-westerly direction until you can take a **sharp left turn**. Follow this path downhill through woodland to the road just above Fingle Bridge.

5 **Turn right** on to the road and follow it past the pub and across the bridge. **Turn right immediately** after the bridge and follow the path along the southern bank of the river. After about 2km **continue** on the path through a gate and then cross the wall on your **right** to reach the suspension footbridge back to the north side of the river and point 3 of the walk. **Turn left** and follow the outbound path back along the river to the A382.

6 Cross the road and continue along the riverbank path to the road by the swimming pool. **Either retrace** the outward route **or turn left** here and follow the road across the bridge and back uphill into Chagford.

FINGLE BRIDGE

15 **Haytor, Hound Tor & Widecombe** 19km/11.8miles

Starting at one of Dartmoor's most iconic tors, visit Hound Tor's medieval houses, the Grimspound stone circles and the pretty village of Widecombe in the Moor.

Haytor Visitor Centre » Haytor Quarries » Smallacombe Rocks » Becca Bridge » Greator Rocks » Hound Tor » Jay's Grave » Grimspound » Hameldown Tor » Hameldown Beacon » Widecombe » Top Tor » Hemsworthy Gate » Saddle Tor » Haytor Rocks » Haytor Visitor Centre

Start
Haytor Visitor Centre. GR: SX 765771.

The Walk

The great, granite knuckle of Haytor, rising from the summit of Haytor Down, is an iconic image of Dartmoor. The 360-degree views from the top (it's an easy scramble to the very top should you wish) take in the surrounding moorland to Hound Tor, the Teign Valley with Castle Drogo in the distance and across the valley to the sea at Torbay.

We begin our walk through the quarries where granite was extracted between 1820 and 1919. Until 1858 the rock was transported on the Haytor Granite Tramway to the Stover Canal and was used for buildings across the country, including the rebuilding of London Bridge. Much of the tramway is still visible, and a long-distance footpath, the Templer Way, follows its former route.

From a high moorland ridge we descend to Becca Brook, crossing on a traditional granite clapper bridge. From here we climb back up to Hound Tor, passing Hound Tor Deserted Medieval Village, a cluster of ruined thirteenth-century barns and long-houses. Hound Tor itself now looms in the distance, said to be the inspiration for Sir Arthur Conan Doyle's *The Hound of the Baskervilles*. Hound Tor and its neighbour Bonehill are popular bouldering venues.

Quiet country lanes lead us to Jay's Grave, a small roadside headstone. Legend has it a local woman, falling upon misfortune, hanged herself at a nearby farm and was buried here in the eighteenth century. There are always fresh flowers upon the grave. Ascending once again on to the high moor we pass Grimspound, a Bronze Age settlement of twenty-four stone hut circles surrounded by a low stone wall. Continuing along the glorious Hameldown Ridge brings us to the village of Widecombe, from where a final climb takes us back over the moor to Haytor.

HAYTOR, HOUND TOR & WIDECOMBE

DISTANCE: 19KM/11.8MILES » **TOTAL ASCENT:** 627M/2,057FT » **START GR:** SX 765771 » **TIME:** ALLOW 5.5 HOURS » **SATNAV:** TQ13 9XS » **MAP:** OS EXPLORER OL28, DARTMOOR, 1:25,000, AND HARVEY SUPERWALKER, DARTMOOR NORTH, 1:25,000 » **REFRESHMENTS:** HOME FARM CAFÉ TRAILER, HAYTOR VISITOR CENTRE CAR PARK; THE RUGGLESTONE INN, WIDECOMBE » **NAVIGATION:** MOSTLY CLEAR PATHS AND SHORT SECTION OF ROAD WITH SOME SECTIONS OF OPEN MOOR. NAVIGATION ON THE OPEN MOOR SECTIONS CAN BECOME TRICKY IN LOW VISIBILITY.

15 HAYTOR, HOUND TOR & WIDECOMBE

Directions — Haytor, Hound Tor & Widecombe

➲ Cross the road and follow a wide path north-west towards the old piles of quarry stone. Pass to the right (east) of the quarry and join a section of the old granite tramway before taking one of the small paths on your **left** heading north. Cross another section of tramway and find the main path (probably **left** on the tramway for a short section) heading north to Smallacombe Rocks.

2 Find the path heading downhill from the north side of the rocks and follow it trending **left** to an open grassy area. Continue downhill into some woodland where the path gets very rocky. Cross the clapper bridge and head steeply uphill through three gates to emerge on to open moor at Greator Rocks.

3 **Continue downhill** initially and then up through a wall, past the medieval village and then up to Hound Tor. Pass between the rocks or to their left and head downhill to the road and car park. **Turn left** on to the road in front of the car park and then **right** at the road junction; follow this road for a little less than 1km to Jay's Grave.

4 **Turn left** and join the path behind the grave heading west over a hill to reach another lane. **Turn left** on the lane and then **almost immediately right** through a gate on to open moor. Follow the track across the stream and then uphill in a north-westerly direction. **Trend right** at the vague path junctions and cross the saddle to drop down slightly to Grimspound.

5 Take the path **left** uphill to the trig point and rocks on Hameldown Tor. Continue heading south along the ridge for about 3km, then take the path heading **left** and downhill, joining a lane and turning **right** into Widecombe.

6 Follow the road east through Widecombe with the church on your right, and continue following the B3387 uphill back on to the moor. Shortly before the top of the hill take a track heading **right** (south-east) from a parking area towards a pile of rocks and then up to Top Tor. Continue past the tor and head downhill to the road junction and cattle grid.

7 Cross the road and follow it east to the car park below Saddle Tor where the road bends to the right. Follow the path uphill here to Saddle Tor and then **continue ahead** towards Haytor. Follow the path around to the **left** of the huge wall of Low Man and continue around until you emerge in the avenue between the two rock exposures. Walk between the rocks and then trend **left** around Haytor and downhill back to the car park.

DARTMOOR PONY NEAR SMALLACOMBE ROCKS

DEWERSTONE ROCK

16 **The Dewerstone & Sheeps Tor**   18.5km/11.5miles

A walk around an intriguing corner of southern Dartmoor, visiting some of the area's most famous granite outcrops and a Spielberg filming location.

Shaugh Prior NT car park » Above the Dewerstone » Wigford Down » Cadover Bridge » River Plym path » Ditsworthy Warren House » Gutter Tor car park » Sheeps Tor » Burrator Reservoir » Meavy » Hoo Meavy » River Meavy path » Shaugh Prior NT car park

Start

Shaugh Prior National Trust car park.
GR: SX 533636.

The Walk

This part of Dartmoor is a delight for those with a passion for outdoor adventure: exciting rivers to paddle, outstanding rock climbing, incredible trail running and, of course, some of the best walking you'll find in the country.

Our route begins near to the Dewerstone, an impressive granite crag shrouded in local myth and legend. 'Dewer' is an ancient Celtic word for the Devil, and it is said he can be seen galloping around the area after dark. Although it is not directly on our route the Dewerstone is well worth a short detour.

Our walk ascends through leafy woodland to the moor above the rocks, the site of an Iron Age hill fort. From here we cross a stretch of high moorland before descending to Cadover Bridge, a popular section of the River Plym with several pools surrounded by open moor. We now follow the Plym as it winds through a landscape dotted with the remnants of ancient settlements to reach Ditsworthy Warren House. This grade II-listed building, originally occupied by the keeper of the local rabbit warren, was used as a location for Steven Spielberg's 2010 film *War Horse*.

From Ditsworthy we climb towards Sheeps Tor, following Edward's Path as it passes Gutter Tor with its 700-year-old unfinished granite cross. After taking in the fine views – on a clear day – from Sheeps Tor we descend to Burrator Reservoir, built in 1898 to supply drinking water to Plymouth and the surrounding towns.

The final stretch of our walk takes in quiet lanes through the moorland towns of Meavy and Hoo Meavy, before following the West Devon Way along the picturesque River Meavy and back to the start.

THE DEWERSTONE & SHEEPS TOR

DISTANCE: 18.5KM/11.5MILES » **TOTAL ASCENT:** 587M/1,926FT » **START GR:** SX 533636 » **TIME:** ALLOW 5.5 HOURS » **SATNAV:** PL7 5HE » **MAP:** OS EXPLORER OL28, DARTMOOR, 1:25,000, AND HARVEY SUPERWALKER, DARTMOOR SOUTH, 1:25,000 » **REFRESHMENTS:** THE ROYAL OAK, MEAVY » **NAVIGATION:** MAINLY STRAIGHTFORWARD ON CLEAR PATHS AND ROAD SECTIONS TOWARDS THE END OF THE ROUTE. THE PATHS CROSS SOME AREAS OF OPEN MOORLAND WHERE CARE IS NEEDED IN POOR VISIBILITY.

**16 THE DEWERSTONE
& SHEEPS TOR**

Directions – The Dewerstone
& Sheeps Tor

➊ Take the path north-east out of the far end of the car park and immediately **turn left** on a path to reach and cross the gated footbridge over the River Plym. Follow the main path uphill and, after a sharp left-hand bend, carry **straight on** along the smaller path and continue uphill above the Dewerstone rocks, emerging on to open moorland. **Continue** north-east up the ridgeline and past some hut circles to reach a crossroads in the path on Wigford Down.

2 **Turn right** and follow the path down towards the River Plym and Cadover Bridge, **turning left** on to the track just before reaching the road. Cross the road just north of the bridge and **continue** on the track heading east then north-east above the River Plym. The track passes several hut circles below Legis Tor before following the river to Ditsworthy Warren House.

3 Follow a bridleway known as Edward's Path north-west from here staying on the south-western bank of the stream and to the west of Eastern Tor to reach the end of the road and Gutter Tor car park. **Turn left** on to the track and follow it across the river and through the car park. **Turn right** on to the track heading north before you get to the cattle grid; follow this track on open moorland around the eastern edge of a series of fields to their most northern corner on Yellowmead Down. **Turn left** here and follow a path west towards the rocky summit of Sheeps Tor.

4 From Sheeps Tor head west downhill in the direction of Burrator Reservoir. **Turn left** at the junction with the bridleway and follow it south along the edge of the woods to the road. **Turn left** and follow the road, then **turn right** at the road junction and follow the road south of the first dam, along the southern shore of the reservoir and across the second dam to reach the western shore of the reservoir.

5 **Turn left** at the road junction after the dam and follow the road south for a short section before you can **turn left** through a gate on to a track heading downhill into some woodland. At the sharp left-hand bend leave the track and take the footpath which continues in the same direction. Follow the path as it curves to the right until it reaches the road at Meavy.

6 **Turn left** on to the road and then take the **first right** along the road through Meavy and past the church. Take the next road **left** signed as National Cycle Network Route 27. Follow this road across the crossroads and through some woods and then downhill to Hoo Meavy. **Turn right** here and follow the road across the River Meavy to reach a stile and gate on your **left** immediately after the bridge.

7 Cross the stile and follow the West Devon Way south along the river to the road bridge at Goodameavy. Continue on the path following the river until you return to the road and car park at the start of the walk.

SHEEPS TOR

SECTION 5

South Devon & the South Hams

The walks in this section explore the South Hams Area of Outstanding Natural Beauty, covering much of the southern peninsula of Devon. Pretty villages and interesting towns nestle within the glorious rolling countryside, while pleasant trails follow the region's rivers as they flow southwards to form a series of picturesque estuaries along the coast. The South West Coast Path rises and falls with the dramatic coastline, dotted with many beaches and sites of historical interest. Rocky headlands reach out into the sea and wildlife abounds year-round in the mild climate.

OUTER HOPE FROM BOLT TAIL

17 Dartington & Berry Pomeroy

22.5km/14miles

A walk through the peaceful countryside that surrounds Totnes and Dartington in the South Devon AONB, visiting a castle and a mansion from medieval times.

Totnes Bridge » John Musgrave Heritage Trail » Gatcombe Brook » Netherton » Berry Pomeroy Castle » Afton » Shadrack » Uphempston » Tallyho » Staverton » Staverton Station » Dartington Hall Estate » NCN Route 2 » Totnes » Totnes Bridge

Start

Totnes Bridge at the east end of Fore Street. GR: SX 806603. (Long-term car parking at Steamer Quay. GR: SX 807599.)

The Walk

Our walk begins in the market town of Totnes, set on the River Dart within the South Devon Area of Outstanding Natural Beauty. Totnes has long had a reputation for its alternative culture, and that is still to be found here, alongside a strong commitment to sustainability – it is both a transition and Fairtrade town. Totnes is said to have more listed buildings per head than any other town, including the Norman motte-and-bailey Totnes Castle, built during the reign of William I, and the Devonian sandstone late-medieval church of St Mary with its thirty-seven-metre-high west tower, visible from afar.

From Totnes we follow the John Musgrave Heritage Trail, a thirty-five-mile long-distance walk that links many of South Devon's finest heritage sites, out to Berry Pomeroy Castle. This Tudor mansion, standing in the grounds of an earlier castle, was built in the fifteenth century by the Pomeroy family. After several changes of hands it was abandoned in the late seventeenth century and is now an atmospheric ruin and a popular tourist attraction owned by English Heritage.

Pleasant walking along quiet lanes and bridleways and a section of leafy woodland brings us to Staverton Station on the South Devon Railway. Steam trains run along here between Buckfastleigh and Totnes on selected days of the year.

From Staverton we follow picturesque trails alongside the River Dart and through the 1,200-acre Dartington Hall estate. The impressive medieval hall at its centre is now the headquarters of the Dartington Hall Trust, a social enterprise that provides training and development in creativity and sustainability. Continuing along the river we join the National Cycle Network to return to Totnes.

DARTINGTON & BERRY POMEROY

DISTANCE: 22.5KM/14MILES » **TOTAL ASCENT:** 524M/1,719FT » **START GR:** SX 806603 » **TIME:** ALLOW 6.5 HOURS » **SATNAV:** TQ9 5AL » **MAP:** OS EXPLORER OL20, SOUTH DEVON, 1:25,000 » **REFRESHMENTS:** RIVERFORD FARM SHOP AND CAFE, STAVERTON » **NAVIGATION:** EASY-TO-FOLLOW PATHS AND ROADS.

**17 DARTINGTON &
BERRY POMEROY**

Directions – Dartington & Berry Pomeroy

⑤ Cross Totnes Bridge heading in an easterly direction away from the town centre. Follow Bridgetown road uphill to reach a junction with the A385. **Turn right** on to the A385 and follow it uphill for 200m before **turning left** on to Bourton Road to join the John Musgrave Heritage Trail (JMHT).

2 Follow this lane uphill for 1.5km; take the **left fork** at the top of the hill, then the **right fork** and then continue across the crossroads to reach the road at Combepark Cross. **Turn left** on to the road and head downhill and across a small bridge. Take the next road **right** and follow it until it takes a sharp left turn. **Turn right** here on to a small lane, recrossing Gatcombe Brook to reach Netherton.

3 **Turn left** here and follow the path (still the JMHT) which follows the brook east through some woodland. Reach and then follow a small lane which crosses the brook and goes past Berry Pomeroy Castle. Continue on the lane to reach a road junction.

4 **Turn left** at the road junction and follow the road taking the **left fork** and heading uphill through Afton. Take the next **left** on to a track past some farm buildings heading west. Follow this to reach the A381. Cross the A381 and follow the lane through Uphempston to reach a **right turn** on to a byway towards Penny's Wood.

5 Follow the byway through the wood and along the river to reach the road at Tallyho. **Turn left** on to the road and under the railway and then **left** across the river bridge and **right** to reach Ford Bridge crossroads (this section of road is busiest at school pickup and drop-off times). Follow the lane signed *Staverton* and continue to follow the signs until you reach the village.

6 **Turn left** on to the road into the village and then **left again** just before the pub, following the road downhill past St Paul's Church to the level crossing. Cross the railway and continue on the lane for a short distance until you can **turn right** on to a footpath near the mill. Follow the path west between the river and the railway to reach the road at Staverton Station. **Turn left** here and follow the lane across the old road bridge and past some houses until you can take a **left turn** on to a track heading east.

7 Follow the main path, **ignoring** the first left but then **keeping left** and following the course of the River Dart around the Dartington estate until you reach the estate road. **Turn left** on to this and follow it through a stone gateway then **turn left** on to a track joining the National Cycle Network (NCN) Route 2.

8 Follow the NCN south into Totnes, crossing the river and railway then reaching the A385. Cross the road here and continue on the NCN heading south, joining Coronation Road and returning to Totnes Bridge.

BERRY POMEROY CASTLE

LOOKING SOUTH-EAST FROM WARREN COTTAGE

18 Noss Mayo

A walk that takes in the pretty South Hams villages of Noss Mayo and Newton Ferrers, peaceful Newton Creek and a dramatic section of the South West Coast Path.

Noss Mayo » Newton Creek » Mouthstone Point » Gara Point » Blackstone Point » Stoke Point » Stoke Church » Beacon Hill » Lambside » Membland » Bridgend » Newton Ferrers » Noss Mayo

Start

Noss Mayo tennis court car park.
GR: SX 547474.

The Walk

Noss Mayo is a picturesque South Hams village arranged along Newton Creek, a tidal arm of the River Yealm estuary. Our walk starts in the centre of the village, following a peaceful lane along the edge of the creek with tantalising glimpses of sparkling blue water and gently rocking boats. We wander through Ferry Wood, emerging as the lane joins the South West Coast Path. From here it's a boat ride if you want to head west, but our walk continues around the headland passing Mouthstone Point, with fine views out towards the Mew Stone and Rame Head.

After rounding the headland at Gara Point the path widens and is known locally as Revelstoke Drive after Lord Revelstoke, the former Baron of Membland (also head of Barings Bank). In the nineteenth century the baron entertained the future King Edward VII at Warren Cottage, which we pass shortly before Blackstone Point, a Site of Special Scientific Interest.

Continuing along the coast path we reach Stoke Point and the remains of Napoleonic and Second World War sea defences. From these dramatic clifftops you can spot rare birds including the cirl bunting, and seals playing in the waves below.

Shortly before leaving the South West Coast Path we arrive at the ruins of Lord Revelstoke's eighteenth-century Beacon Hill Tea House, now owned by the Carswell Estate. From here we head inland to Membland, following Newton Creek to Newton Ferrers. The road between the two villages is always passable, however the most enjoyable route crosses the tidal causeway at low tide, returning us to Noss Mayo.

If you're staying in the area and fancy a trip from Noss Mayo across the Yealm Estuary to Wembury, a passenger ferry operates between April and September.

NOSS MAYO

DISTANCE: 15.8KM/9.8MILES » **TOTAL ASCENT:** 537M/1,762FT » **START GR:** SX 547474 » **TIME:** ALLOW 5 HOURS » **SATNAV:** PL8 1EH » **MAP:** OS EXPLORER OL20, SOUTH DEVON, 1:25,000 » **REFRESHMENTS:** THE SHIP INN, NOSS MAYO » **NAVIGATION:** CLEAR COAST PATH, BYWAY AND SECTIONS OF QUIET ROAD.

18 NOSS MAYO

Directions – Noss Mayo

⑤▸ **Turn right** out of the car park and then take the **first left** on to a narrow lane; follow this for a short distance and then **turn right** on to Foundry Lane and follow this down to the road and car park at the mouth of the creek. **Turn left** on to this road (Passage Road) and follow it past the Ship Inn and around a left-hand bend following the course of the river. A path that runs through National Trust woodland on your left, parallel to the lane, is a pleasant alternative to walking on the road. **Fork right** following *South West Coast Path* signs and follow the lane on to the coast path.

2 Follow the SWCP around Mouthstone Point and then Gara Point and continue now heading south-east past Blackstone Point to Stoke Point. Continue on the SWCP as it travels north above Stoke Beach caravan park and crosses a minor road. Carry on now walking east to reach the ruined eighteenth-century tea house on Beacon Hill.

3 Follow the SWCP down the steep field and then up a steep track. **Turn left** off the SWCP shortly after the top of the hill and follow the path north-west to reach a road. **Turn right** on to the road and then **left** on to the next minor road. After a short distance on the road take the byway **right** and follow this downhill to a T-junction. **Turn left** here and follow the track west to reach the road in Membland.

4 **Turn right** and follow the road downhill to the road junction and bridge at the east end of Newton Creek. *If the tide is low **turn right** here and follow the road along the north side of the creek **staying left** when the main road turns right uphill and following the creek to the pedestrian crossing point. Cross here and follow the beach around to the **right** to reach a small stone pier. Drop down on to the beach again and cross the southern arm of the creek to reach the road. **Turn left** here and retrace the outward route.

*OR If the tide is high follow the road **left** on the southern bank of the creek. **Fork right** on to Pillory Hill and follow this around past the Swan Inn to reach a road junction. **Turn right** here and then **immediately left** back up Foundry Lane and retrace the outward route back to the start.

VIEW OF NEWTON FERRERS ACROSS NEWTON CREEK

SOUTH WEST COAST PATH LOOKING EAST FROM BOLBERRY DOWN

19 **Bolt Tail & Bolt Head**

17.8km/11.1miles

A walk out through the peaceful South Hams countryside and back along a breathtaking section of the South West Coast Path between Bolt Head and Bolt Tail.

Outer Hope » Inner Hope » Burton Ridges » Malborough » Combe » Splatcove Point » Bolt Head » Bolberry Down » Bolt Tail » Inner Hope » Outer Hope

Start

Outer Hope car park. GR: SX 675401.

The Walk

Our walk begins in the thatched village of Outer Hope, passing the sandy beach at Hope Cove. The rocky fingers that reach treacherously into the sea have wrecked many ships here, and the area gained a reputation for plundering and smuggling. There has been a lifeboat station at Hope Cove intermittently since 1878 and the one today exists on charitable donations with the support of the village. There have been five boats in the history of the station, all called *Alexandra*.

From here we continue through Inner Hope, taking in the peaceful lanes and windswept fields that characterise this part of the South Hams. Look out for kestrels and peregrines hunting from above and flocks of rare cirl buntings which are only found in this part of the UK. Reaching Malborough, we pass the thirteenth-century All Saints church, built from local

Soar stone, whose tall spire can be seen from miles around.

Our walk continues through woodland, fields and lanes to eventually join the South West Coast Path near to Overbeck's, the seaside home of the early twentieth-century scientist and inventor Otto Overbeck (National Trust owned).

Next, we arrive at the dramatic jagged rocks that mark Bolt Head. From here, breathtaking views stretch from Dodman Point in the west to Prawle Point in the east. Our walk now follows the glorious stretch of the South West Coast Path that runs between here and Bolt Tail. We pass the secluded sandy beach at Soar Mill Cove and the wild headland of Bolberry Down, a Site of Special Scientific Interest.

The final section of our walk brings us to Bolt Tail where, some sixty metres above the waves, stand the remains of an Iron Age hill fort, a perfect place to pause and take in the views.

BOLT TAIL & BOLT HEAD

DISTANCE: 17.8KM/11.1MILES » **TOTAL ASCENT:** 484M/1,588FT » **START GR:** SX 675401 » **TIME:** ALLOW 5.5 HOURS » **SATNAV:** TQ7 3HQ » **MAP:** OS EXPLORER OL20, SOUTH DEVON, 1:25,000 » **REFRESHMENTS:** THE COVE CAFE, HOPE COVE » **NAVIGATION:** STRAIGHTFORWARD COAST PATH AND INLAND PATHS AND LANES.

71

19 BOLT TAIL & BOLT HEAD

Directions – Bolt Tail & Bolt Head

➎ Walk south on the South West Coast Path past the harbour and along a footpath below some cottages. **Turn left** when you reach the end of a lane and head uphill on a footpath to reach a road; cross this and follow the lane heading slightly uphill. This turns into a footpath called Burton Ridges; follow this due east across several fields to reach another lane.

2 **Turn right** on to the road and follow it into Malborough. Walk past the church and **fork right** on to Lower Town. Take the **second right** on to Well Hill and join the footpath heading across fields in a south-easterly direction. Pass Portlemore Barton on a lane taking the **left fork** and following the stream in the same direction past a small wood to reach another lane. **Bear right** and **continue** on the lane south-east through Combe and take the footpath on the **left** into the woods; follow this in the same direction down towards the mouth of the estuary. The path curves to the left and joins the end of Moult Road; follow this and **fork right** where it joins the main road.

3 **Turn right** on to the road where you join the South West Coast Path heading south. Follow the road around Splatcove Point and join the path where the road ends heading towards Bolt Head. From Bolt Head continue on the SWCP in a north-westerly direction all the way to Bolt Tail.

4 Continue on the SWCP heading downhill in a north-easterly direction to emerge by the lifeboat station in Inner Hope. **Turn left** on to the coastal road and head uphill; **stay left** to join the outbound path back to Outer Hope and the end of the walk.

HOPE COVE FROM BOLT TAIL

VIEW SOUTH FROM BEESANDS TOWARDS START POINT

20 Start Point, Prawle Point & Gammon Head

22.8km/14.2miles

Explore the windswept headlands, coastal villages and secluded beaches dotted along the most southerly reaches of Devon.

Beesands » Hallsands » Start Point » Lannacombe Bay » Prawle Point » Gara Rock » West Prawle » Cousin's Cross » Huccombe » Beesands

Start
Beesands. GR: SX 820406.

The Walk

The small fishing village of Beesands lies on the coast of Start Bay in the very southern-most part of Devon. Beesands Ley, a wild-life-rich freshwater lake, lies behind the beach – a smaller version of the better-known Slapton Ley further north. The village pub, The Cricket Inn, was the venue of Keith Richards and Mick Jagger's first live gig.

From Beesands we follow the South West Coast Path past the village of Hallsands. In 1917 storms destroyed all but one house here after breaching the sea defences. The disaster was blamed on the extraction of thousands of tons of gravel from the Sker-ries Bank just off Hallsands, used to build Plymouth's naval dockyard. Recent storms have removed more gravel from the beach leaving its peat beds exposed, and once again the future of the village – and much of this stretch of coastline – looks uncertain.

Continuing along the coast path we arrive at Start Point, a spectacular rocky headland and, along with its neighbour Prawle Point further west, one of the most southerly points in Devon. Start Point lighthouse was built in 1836 to warn ships away from the many treacherous rocks that lie submerged around the bay. The lighthouse is open to the public on selected days each year (paid entry).

Rounding the headland brings us to Lan-nacombe Bay, a secluded sandy beach sur-rounded by rocky outcrops that's enjoyable to explore. Further on lies Prawle Point, another craggy headland with spectacular views, and Pig's Nose, the site of an unsuccessful iron mine in the mid-nineteenth century.

At Gara Rock we leave the coast path and head inland, following a route through the peaceful, undulating South Devon hills on lanes, tracks and fields to return to the coast and Beesands village.

START POINT, PRAWLE POINT & GAMMON HEAD

DISTANCE: 22.8KM/14.2MILES » **TOTAL ASCENT:** 637M/2,090FT » **START GR:** SX 820406 » **TIME:** ALLOW 8 HOURS » **SATNAV:** TQ7 2EH » **MAP:** OS EXPLORER OL20, SOUTH DEVON, 1:25,000 » **REFRESHMENTS:** BRITANNIA @ THE BEACH & THE CRICKET INN, BEESANDS » **NAVIGATION:** CLEAR COAST PATH, BYWAY AND SECTIONS OF QUIET ROAD.

CONT. ON PAGE 143

20 START POINT, PRAWLE POINT & GAMMON HEAD

DEVON FLAG FLYING IN BEESANDS

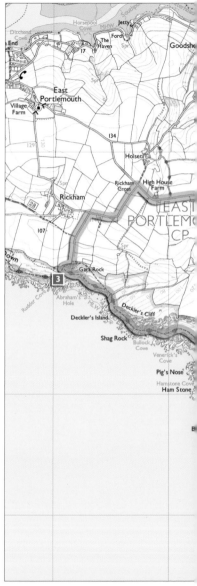

CONT. ON PAGE 140

STARTS ON PAGE 141

Wilton

Northern Town Farm

Chivelstone

South Allington

NTL

Ford

est Waterhead

4

West Prawle Wood
108

Chivelstone Cross
87

Pitt's Plantation

CHIVELSTONE CP

est Prawle Farm

Walland

Higher Borough
127

Lower Borough

Lannacombe Barn

Lannacombe Cottage

Moor Farm

28

138

Knowle Fork

Woodcombe

Vinivers Cross

Tumulus

Wr Twr

138

Higher House Farm

134

Coolings Farm

Woodcombe Point

Woodcombe Sand
Long Cove

Evator Cove

Grant's Rock

Ballsaddle Rock

East Prawle

Higher Farm

PC

The Torrs

Hines Hill

Maelcombe House

Stinking Cove

114

Malcombe Point

Gorah Run

Gorah Rocks

74

Horseley Cove

Sharpers Head

Sharpers Cove

Dutch End

Elender Cove

90
Signalhouse Point

P

Fish-in-the-Well Rock

Lobeater Rock

Brimpool Rocks

Meg Rock

Black Cove

S W C Path

Langerstone Point

Lookout Station

Landing Cove

Maelcombe Cove

Copstone Cove

Prawle Point

20 START POINT, PRAWLE POINT & GAMMON HEAD

Directions – Start Point, Prawle Point & Gammon Head

➡ Head south along the seafront and on to the South West Coast Path. Follow the path, which runs across some fields and along the side of the hill, to the stony beach at Hallsands. Continue south on the SWCP towards the lighthouse on Start Point. The SWCP doesn't actually go to the lighthouse but it's a pleasant detour.

2 Continue on the rocky SWCP in a westerly direction, above and below some cliffs and then along the edge of several fields around Lannacombe Bay to reach Prawle Point. Continue on the SWCP now in a north-westerly direction to Gara Rock.

3 **Turn right** and leave the coast path, heading inland past the Gara Rock hotel and following the lane north. Take the **first right** and then follow the lane to the next junction. **Turn right** on to the next lane and follow it to West Prawle. Leave the road **left** at the sharp right turn and follow the bridleway on a track. Follow the bridleway across some fields and through some woodland to reach another road.

4 **Turn right** on to the road and follow it for about 500m. Take the **first right turn** and then **turn left** on to a byway. Follow this to the next road. **Turn left** on to the road and follow it for a short distance to where you can **turn right** on to another byway. Follow this across a field to reach another road. **Turn right** on to the road and follow it across Cousin's Cross in a north-easterly direction.

5 The lane ends at a five-way road junction called Dunstone Cross. Cross the road and head downhill on the lane to Huccombe. Take the next **left** then **keep right** staying on the main road. **Turn right** at the next junction and then follow the main road **left** and downhill to Beesands.

DAY WALKS GUIDEBOOKS

Written by local authors, each pocket-sized guidebook features:

- 20 great day-length walks
- Ordnance Survey 1:25,000-scale maps
- easy-to-follow directions
- distance & navigation information
- refreshment stops & local area information
- detailed appendix

available 2018

1 **DAY WALKS IN SCOTLAND**

2 **DAY WALKS IN SNOWDONIA**

3 **DAY WALKS IN THE BRECON BEACONS**

4 **DAY WALKS ON THE PEMBROKESHIRE COAST**

5 **DAY WALKS IN THE LAKE DISTRICT**

6 **DAY WALKS IN THE YORKSHIRE DALES**

7 **DAYS WALKS IN THE NORTH YORK MOORS**

8 **DAY WALKS IN THE PEAK DISTRICT**

9 **DAY WALKS IN THE PEAK DISTRICT**

10 **DAY WALKS IN THE COTSWOLDS**

11 **DAY WALKS IN DEVON**

12 **DAY WALKS ON THE SOUTH DOWNS**

Available from book shops or direct from:
www.v-publishing.co.uk

A complete list of good places to eat and stay
in Devon is beyond the scope of this book –
in fact there are books dedicated to the subject
– however the following list represents a small
sample that we have tried and tested, or for
which we have received reliable recommendations.

Tourist Information Centres

www.visitdevon.co.uk
www.visitsouthdevon.co.uk
www.northdevon.com
www.visitdartmoor.co.uk

Ashburton	T: 01364 653 426
Bovey Tracey	T: 01626 832 047
Buckfastleigh	T: 01364 644 522
Dartmouth	T: 01803 834 224
Exeter	T: 01392 665 700
Kingsbridge	T: 01548 853 195
Modbury	T: 01548 830 159
Salcombe	T: 01548 843 927
Seaton	T: 01297 300 390
Tiverton	T: 01884 230 878

Food and Drink
Cafes and Restaurants

Charlie Friday's
Lynton — T: 07544 123 324
Cheristow Lavender Tea Room
Hartland — T:01237 440 101
(also campsite and gardens)
Home Farm Café (also a trailer at Haytor car park)
Bovey Tracey — T: 01626 830 016
National Trust Tea Rooms
Lydford Gorge — T: 01822 820 320
Ben's Farm Shop and Cafe
Staverton — T: 01803 762 851

Ben's Farm Shop and Cafe
Yealmpton — T: 01752 880 925
Britannia @ the Beach
Beesands — T: 01548 581 168
The Pelican Fish and Chip Restaurant
Barnstaple — T: 01271 345 605
Darts Farm Cafe and Deli
Topsham — T: 01392 878 200
Sandleigh Tea Room and Garden
Croyde Bay — T: 01271 890 930
Kirsty's Kitchen
North Tawton — T: 01837 880 366
The Sea Shanty Beach Café
Branscombe — T: 01297 680 577
The Cove
Hope Cove — T: 01548 561 376
Beach House
South Milton — T: 01548 561 144
Barricane Beach Cafe
Woolacombe — T: 07969 189 304
The Oyster Shack
Bigbury — T: 01548 810 876
National Trust Cafe
Killerton — T: 01392 881 345

Pubs

The Dartmoor Inn
Lydford — T: 01822 820 221
The Blue Ball Inn
Countisbury — T: 01598 741 263
The Rams Head Inn
Dolton (also rooms) — T: 01805 804 255
The Royal Oak
Meavy — T: 01822 852 944
The Sir Walter Raleigh
East Budleigh — T: 01395 442 510
The Culm Valley Inn
Culmstock — T: 01884 840 354

The Rugglestone Inn
Widecombe in the Moor — T: 01364 621 327

The Duke of York
Iddesleigh — T: 01837 810 253

The Ship Inn
Noss Mayo — T: 01752 872 387

The Masons Arms
Branscombe (also rooms) — T: 01297 680 300

The Fountain Head
Branscombe — T: 01297 680 359

The Bridge Inn
Topsham — T: 01392 873 862

The Pigs Nose Inn
East Prawle — T: 01548 511 209

Accommodation
Bothies, Bunkhouses and Hostels

National Trust

Peppercombe Bothy — T: 0344 800 2070
Foreland Bothy — T: 0344 800 2070
Foreland Bunkhouse — T: 0344 800 2070

YHA youth hostels can be found at the following locations in Devon. For details and booking please visit: **www.yha.org.uk**

Beer — T: 0345 371 9502
Dartmoor — T: 0345 371 9622
Elmscott, nr Hartland — T: 01237 441 276
Exford — T: 0800 019 1700
Minehead — T: 0345 371 9033
Okehampton — T: 01837 539 16
Okehampton Bracken Tor — T: 01837 539 16

Self-catering, B&Bs and Hotels

North Walk House
Lynton (B&B and SC) — T: 01598 753 372

The Linhay
Copplestone, Crediton — T: 01363 843 86

The Rams Head Inn
Dolton — T: 01805 804 255

Witherdon Wood
Shepherd's Hut — T: 01837 871 123

Carswell Farm holiday cottages
Holbeton — T: 01752 830 020

Wheatland Farm Eco Lodges
Winkleigh — T: 01837 834 99

The Masons Arms
Branscombe — T: 01297 680 300

South Sands Hotel
Bolt Head — T: 01548 845 900

Lewtrenchard Manor Hotel
Okehampton — T: 01566 783 222

Crenham Eyrie
Hartland — T: 01288 331 150

Camping

Stoke Barton Farm Campsite
Hartland — T: 01237 441 238

Coombe View Farm
Branscombe — T: 01297 680 218

Cloud Farm
Doone Valley, Exmoor — T: 01598 741 278

Roadford Lake Campsite — T: 01566 771 930

Karrageen Camping
Bolberry — T: 01548 561 230

Beryl's Field
Beeson — T: 07967 116 682

Langstone Manor
nr Tavistock — T: 01822 613 371

Cockingford Farm
nr Widecombe in the Moor — T: 01364 621 258

Wild camping on Dartmoor – allowed in certain areas. Please check national park guidelines.

Outdoor Shops

Taunton Leisure, Exeter
T: 01392 410 534   www.tauntonleisure.com

Cotswold Outdoor, Darts Farm, Topsham nr Exeter
T: 01392 878 313 www.cotswoldoutdoor.com

Cotswold Outdoor, Plymouth
T: 01752 672 024 www.cotswoldoutdoor.com

Go Outdoors, Plymouth
T: 01344 387 6835   www.gooutdoors.co.uk

Weather

www.metoffice.gov.uk

Other Publications

Day Walks in the Cotswolds
Judy Mills, Vertebrate Publishing –
www.v-publishing.co.uk

Day Walks in the Brecon Beacons
Harri Roberts, Vertebrate Publishing –
www.v-publishing.co.uk

Day Walks on the South Downs
Deirdre Huston, Vertebrate Publishing –
www.v-publishing.co.uk

South West Mountain Biking
Nick Cotton, Vertebrate Publishing –
www.v-publishing.co.uk

About the Authors

Jen and Sim Benson are passionate about exploring wild places, whether they're running through the mountains, walking the National Trails or climbing on their local Dartmoor granite. In 2015 they spent a year living under canvas in Britain with their two young children. They are the authors of the guidebook *Wild Running* and the National Trust book *Amazing Family Adventures*, and are regular contributors to a wide range of outdoor publications, as well as routes editors and gear testers for *Trail Running* magazine. www.jenandsimbenson.co.uk

Vertebrate Publishing

At Vertebrate Publishing we publish books to inspire adventure. It's our rule that the only books we publish are those that we'd want to read or use ourselves. We endeavour to bring you beautiful books that stand the test of time and that you'll be proud to have on your bookshelf for years to come. www.v-publishing.co.uk